My Life

and

My Life

in the

Nineties

Wesleyan Poetry

My Life and My Life in the Nineties

Lyn Hejinian

Wesleyan University Press | Middletown, Connecticut

Wesleyan University Press

Middletown CT 06459

www.wesleyan.edu/wespress

© 2013, 2003, 1987, 1980 Lyn Hejinian

All rights reserved

Manufactured in the United States of America

Designed by Mindy Basinger Hill

Typeset in Bauer Bodoni

Wesleyan University Press is a member of the
Green Press Initiative. The paper used in this book
meets their minimum requirement for recycled paper.

Library of Congress Cataloging-in-Publication Data

Hejinian, Lyn.

My life and My life in the nineties / Lyn Hejinian.

        p.   cm. — (Wesleyan poetry)

ISBN 978-0-8195-7351-3 (pbk. : alk. paper) —

ISBN 978-0-8195-7352-0 (eBook)

I. Hejinian, Lyn. My life in the nineties. II. Title.

III. Title: My life and My life in the nineties.

PS3558.E4735M93 2013

811'.54 — dc23   2012028825

5   4   3   2

For LMO—

continuity between

the words

Contents

Acknowledgments   The original, thirty-seven-part version of *My Life* was published by Burning Deck in 1980. A second, expanded (forty-five-part) version of the work was published in 1987 by Sun & Moon Press and subsequently by Green Integer. The author most sincerely thanks Rosmarie and Keith Waldrop of Burning Deck for their support of that first appearance of the work and for their friendship through all the years since. The importance of Douglas Messerli's dedication to the world of innovative writing cannot be overestimated, and his support of *My Life* in that context and others is here very gratefully acknowledged.

My Life in the Nineties was written expressly for Shark Books, which published it in 2003. It is but one manifestation of an ongoing creative camaraderie between the author and Emilie Clark and Lytle Shaw.

My Life

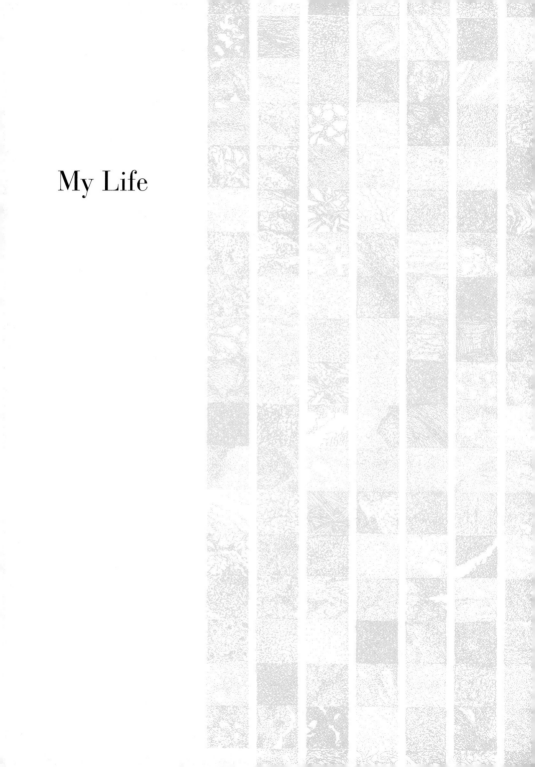

A pause, a rose,
something on paper

A moment yellow, just as four years later, when my father returned home from the war, the moment of greeting him, as he stood at the bottom of the stairs, younger, thinner than when he had left, was purple—though moments are no longer so colored. Somewhere, in the background, rooms share a pattern of small roses. Pretty is as pretty does. In certain families, the meaning of necessity is at one with the sentiment of pre-necessity. The better things were gathered in a pen. The windows were narrowed by white gauze curtains which were never loosened. Here I refer to irrelevance, that rigidity which never intrudes. Hence, repetitions, free from all ambition. The shadow of the redwood trees, she said, was oppressive. The plush must be worn away. On her walks she stepped into people's gardens to pinch off cuttings from their geraniums and succulents. An occasional sunset is reflected on the windows. A little puddle is overcast. If only you could touch, or, even, catch those gray great creatures. I was afraid of my uncle with the wart on his nose, or of his jokes at our expense which were beyond me, and I was shy of my aunt's deafness who was his sister-in-law and who had years earlier fallen into the habit of nodding, agreeably. Wool station. See lightning, wait for thunder. Quite mistakenly, as it happened. Long time lines trail behind every idea, object, person, pet, vehicle, and event. The afternoon happens, crowded and therefore endless. Thicker, she agreed. It was a tic, she had the habit, and now she bobbed like my toy plastic bird on the edge of its glass, dipping into and recoiling from the water. But a word is a bottomless pit. It became magically pregnant and one day split open, giving birth to a stone egg, about as big as a football. In May when the lizards emerge from the stones, the stones turn gray, from green. When daylight moves, we delight in distance. The waves rolled over our stomachs, like spring rain over an orchard slope. Rubber bumpers on rubber cars. The resistance on sleeping to being asleep. In every country is a word which attempts the sound of cats, to match an inisolable portrait in the clouds to a din in the air. But the constant noise is not an omen of music to come. "Everything is a question of sleep," says Cocteau, but he forgets the shark, which does not. Anxiety is vigilant. Perhaps initially, even before one can talk, restlessness is already conventional, establishing the incoherent border which will later separate events from experience. Find a drawer that's not filled up. That we sleep plunges our work into the dark. The ball was lost in a bank of myrtle. I was in a room with the particulars of which a later nostalgia might be formed, an indulged childhood. They are sitting in wicker chairs, the legs of which have sunk unevenly into the ground, so that each is sitting slightly tilted and their postures make adjustment for that. The cows warm their own barn. I look at them fast and it gives the illusion that they're moving. An "oral history" on paper. *That* morning this morning. I say it about the psyche because it is not optional. The overtones are a denser shadow in the room characterized by its habitual readiness, a form of charged waiting, a perpetual attendance, of which I was thinking when I began the paragraph, "So much of childhood is spent in a manner of waiting."

You spill the sugar when you lift the spoon. My father had filled an old apothecary jar with what he called "sea glass," bits of old bottles rounded and textured by the sea, so abundant on beaches. There is no solitude. It buries itself in veracity. It is as if one splashed in the water lost by one's tears. My mother had climbed into the garbage can in order to stamp down the accumulated trash, but the can was knocked off balance, and when she fell she broke her arm. She could only give a little shrug. The family had little money but plenty of food. At the circus only the elephants were greater than anything I could have imagined. The egg of Columbus, landscape and grammar. She wanted one where the playground was dirt, with grass, shaded by a tree, from which would hang a rubber tire as a swing, and when she found it she sent me. These creatures are compound and nothing they do should surprise us. I don't mind, or I won't mind, where the verb "to care" might multiply. The pilot of the little airplane had forgotten to notify the airport of his approach, so that when the lights of the plane in the night were first spotted, the air raid sirens went off, and the entire city on that coast went dark. He was taking a drink of water and the light was growing dim. My mother stood at the window watching the only lights that were visible, circling over the darkened city in search of the hidden airport. Unhappily, time seems more normative than place. Whether breathing or holding the breath, it was the same thing, driving through the tunnel from one sun to the next under a hot brown hill. She sunned the baby for sixty seconds, leaving him naked except for a blue cotton sunbonnet. At night, to close off the windows from view of the street, my grandmother pulled down the window shades, never loosening the curtains, a gauze starched too stiff to hang properly down. I sat on

(5

the windowsill singing sunny lunny teena, ding-dang-dong. Out there is an aging magician who needs a tray of ice in order to turn his bristling breath into steam. He broke the radio silence. Why would anyone find astrology interesting when it is possible to learn about astronomy. What one passes in the Plymouth. It is the wind slamming the doors. All that is nearly incommunicable to my friends. Velocity and throat verisimilitude. Were we seeing a pattern or merely an appearance of small white sailboats on the bay, floating at such a distance from the hill that they appeared to be making no progress. And for once to a country that did not speak another language. To follow the progress of ideas, or that particular line of reasoning, so full of surprises and unexpected correlations, was somehow to take a vacation. Still, you had to wonder where they had gone, since you could speak of reappearance. A blue room is always dark. Everything on the boardwalk was shooting toward the sky. It was not specific to any year, but very early. A German goldsmith covered a bit of metal with cloth in the fourteenth century and gave humankind its first button. It was hard to know this as politics, because it plays like the work of one person, but nothing is isolated in history—certain humans are situations. Are your fingers in the margin. Their random procedures make monuments to fate. There is something still surprising when the green emerges. The blue fox has ducked its head. The front rhyme of harmless with harmony. Where is my honey running. You cannot linger "on the lamb." You cannot determine the nature of progress until you assemble all of the relatives.

It seemed that we had hardly begun and we were already there

We see only the leaves and branches of the trees close in around the house. Those submissive games were sensual. I was no more than three or four years old, but when crossed I would hold my breath, not from rage but from stubbornness, until I lost consciousness. The shadows one day deeper. Every family has its own collection of stories, but not every family has someone to tell them. In a small studio in an old farmhouse, it is the musical expression of a glowing optimism. A bird would reach but be secret. Absence of allusion: once, and ring alone. The downstairs telephone was in a little room as dark as a closet. It made a difference between the immediate and the sudden in a theater filled with transitions. Without what can a person function as the sea functions without me. A typical set of errands. My mother stood between us and held our hands as we waded into the gray-blue water, lecturing us on the undertow, more to add to the thrill of the approaching water than to warn us of any real danger, since she would continue to grip us by the hand when the wave came in and we tried to jump over it. The curve of the rain, more, comes over more often. Four seasons circle a square year. A mirror set in the crotch of the tree was like a hole in the out-of-doors. I could have ridden in the car forever, or so it seemed, watching the scenery go by, alert as to the circumstances of a dream, and that peaceful. Roller coast. The fog lifts a late sunrise. There are floral twigs in position on it. The roots of the locust tree were lifting the corner of the little cabin. Our unease grows before the newly restless. There you are, and you know it's good, and all you have to do is make it better. He sailed to the war. A life no more free than the life of a lost puppy. It became popular and then we were inundated with imitations. My old aunt entertained us with her lie, a story about an event in her girlhood, a catastrophe in a sailboat that never occurred, but she was blameless, unaccountable, since, in the course of the telling, she had come to believe the lie herself. A kind of burbling in the waters of inspiration. Because of their recurrence, what had originally seemed merely details of atmosphere became, in time, thematic. As if sky plus sun *must* make leaves. A snapdragon volunteering in the garden among the cineraria gapes its maw between the fingers, and we pinched the buds of the fuchsia to make them pop. Is that willful. Inclines. They have big calves because of those hills. Flip over small stones, dried mud. We thought that the mica might be gold. A pause, a rose, something on paper, in a nature scrapbook. What follows a strict chronology has no memory. For me, they must exist, the contents of that absent reality, the objects and occasions which now I reconsidered. The smells of the house were thus a peculiar mix of heavy interior air and the air from outdoors lingering over the rose bushes, the camellias, the hydrangeas, the rhododendron and azalea bushes. Hard to distinguish hunger from wanting to eat. My grandmother was in the kitchen, her hands on her hips, wearing what she called a "wash dress," watching a line of ants cross behind the faucets of the sink, and she said to us, "Now *I* am waging war." There are strings in the terrible distance. They are against the blue. The trees are continually receiving their own shadows.

A name trimmed
with colored ribbons

They are seated in the shadows husking corn, shelling peas. Houses of wood set in the ground. I try to find the spot at which the pattern on the floor repeats. Pink, and rosy, quartz. They wade in brackish water. The leaves outside the window tricked the eye, demanding that one see them, focus on them, making it impossible to look past them, and though holes were opened through the foliage, they were as useless as portholes underwater looking into a dark sea, which only reflect the room one seeks to look out from. Sometimes into benevolent and other times into ghastly shapes. It speaks of a few of the rather terrible blind. I grew stubborn until blue as the eyes overlooking the bay from the bridge scattered over its bowls through a fading light and backed by the protest of the bright breathless West. Each bit of Jell-O had been molded in tiny doll dishes, each trembling orange bit a different shape, but all otherwise the same. I am urged out rummaging into the sunshine, and the depths increase of blue above. A paper hat afloat on a cone of water. The orange and gray bugs were linked from their mating but faced in opposite directions, and their scrambling amounted to nothing. This simply means that the imagination is more restless than the body. But, already, words. Can there be laughter without comparisons. The tongue lisps in its hilarious panic. If, for example, you say, "I always prefer being by myself," and, then, one afternoon, you want to telephone a friend, maybe you feel you have betrayed your ideals. We have poured into the sink the stale water in which the iris died. Life is hopelessly frayed, all loose ends. A pansy suddenly, a web, a trail remarkably's a snail's. It was an enormous egg, sitting in the vineyard—an enormous rock-shaped egg. On that still day my grandmother raked up the leaves beside a particular pelargonium. With a name like that there is a lot you can

(9

do. Children are not always inclined to choose such paths. You can tell by the eucalyptus tree, its shaggy branches scatter buttons. In the afternoons, when the shades were pulled for my nap, the light coming through was of a dark yellow, nearly orange, melancholy, as heavy as honey, and it made me thirsty. That doesn't say it all, nor even a greater part. Yet it seems even more incomplete when we were there in person. Half the day in half the room. The wool makes one itch and the scratching makes one warm. But herself that she obeyed she dressed. It talks. The baby is scrubbed everywhere, he is an apple. They are true kitchen stalwarts. The smell of breathing fish and breathing shells seems sad, a mystery, rapturous, then dead. A self-centered being, in this different world. A urinating doll, half-buried in sand. She is lying on her stomach with one eye closed, driving a toy truck along the road she has cleared with her fingers. I mean untroubled by the distortions. That was the fashion when she was a young woman and famed for her beauty, surrounded by beaux. Once it was circular and that shape can still be seen from the air. Protected by the dog. Protected by foghorns, frog honks, cricket circles on the brown hills. It was a message of happiness by which we were called into the room, as if to receive a birthday present given early, because it was too large to hide, or alive, a pony perhaps, his mane trimmed with colored ribbons.

What is the meaning
hung from that depend

A dog bark, the engine of a truck, an airplane hidden by the trees and rooftops. My mother's childhood seemed a kind of holy melodrama. She ate her pudding in a pattern, carving a rim around the circumference of the pudding, working her way inward toward the center, scooping with the spoon, to see how far she could separate the pudding from the edge of the bowl before the center collapsed, spreading the pudding out again, lower, back to the edge of the bowl. You could tell that it was improvisational because at that point they closed their eyes. A pause, a rose, something on paper. Solitude was the essential companion. The branches of the redwood trees hung in a fog whose moisture they absorbed. Lasting, "what might be," its present a future, like the life of a child. The greatest solitudes are quickly strewn with rubbish. All night the radio covered the fall of a child in the valley down an abandoned well-fitting, a clammy narrow pipe fifty-six feet deep, in which he was wedged, recorded, and died. Stanza there. The synchronous, which I have characterized as spatial, is accurate to reality but it has been debased. Daisy's plenty pebbles in the gravel drive. It is a tartan not a plaid. There was some disparity between my grandfather's reserve, the result of shyness and disdain, and his sense that a man's natural importance was characterized by bulk, by the great depth of his footprint in the sand—in other words, a successful man was no lightweight. A flock of guard geese are pecking in a cold rain, become formal behind the obvious flower's bloom. The room, in fact, was used as a closet as well, for as one sat at the telephone table, one faced a row of my grandparents' overcoats, raincoats, and hats, which were hung from a line of heavy, polished wooden hooks. The fog burned off and I went for a walk alone, then was lost between the grapevines, unable to return, until they set a mast,   *(11* a pole, into the ground and hung up a colored flag that I could see from anywhere around. A glass snail was set among real camellias in a glass bowl upon the table. Pure duration, a compound plenum in which nothing is repeated. Photographed in a blue pinafore. The way Dorothy Wordsworth often, I think, went out to "get" a sight. But language is restless. They say there has been too much rough-housing. The heat waves wobbled over the highway — on either side were flat brown fields tilted slightly toward the horizon — and in the distance ahead of the car small blue ponds lay in our path, evaporating suddenly, as if in a single piece, at the instant prior to our splashing in. I saw a line of rocks topped by a foghorn protecting the little harbor from the tide. Fruit peels and the heels of bread were left to get moldy. But then we'd need, what, a bird, to eat the fleas from the rug. When what happens is not intentional, one can't ascribe meaning to it, and unless what happens is necessary, one can't expect it to occur again. Because children will spill food, one needs a dog. Rubber books for bathtubs. Coast laps. One had merely to turn around in order to see it. Elbows off the table. The portrait, a photograph, had been made so that my grandmother was looking just over the head of the observer, into a little distance, not so far as to be a space into which she might seem to be staring, but at some definite object, some noun, just behind one. Waffle men everywhere. She had come upon a set of expressions ("peachy" being one of them and "nuts to you" another) which exactly suited her, and so, though the expressions went out of everyone else's vocabulary, even years later, when everyone else was saying "far out" or "that's nowhere," she continued to have a "perfectly peachy time" on her vacations. This was Melody Ranch, daring and resourceful. As for we who "love to be astonished," we might go to the zoo and see the famous hippo named "Bubbles." The side saddle was impossible, and yet I've seen it used successfully, even stunningly, the woman's full skirts spread like a wing as the horse jumped a hurdle and they galloped on. Lasting, ferries, later, trolleys from Berkeley to the Bridge. This is one of those things which continues, and hence seems important, and so ever what one says over and over again. Soggy sky, which then dries out, lifting slightly turning white — and then banks toward the west. If I see fishing boats that's the first thing I think. Insane, in common parlance.

It was a mountain creek, running over little pebbles of white quartz and mica. Let's say that every possibility waits. In raga time is added to measure, which expands. A deep thirst, faintly smelling of artichoke hearts, and resembling the sleepiness of childhood. At every birthday party that year, the mother of the birthday child served ice cream and "surprise cake," into whose slices the "favors" were baked. But nothing could interrupt those given days. I was sipping Shirley Temples wearing my Mary Janes. My grandfather was as serious as any general before any battle, though he had been too young for the First War and too old for the Second. He carried not a cane but a walking stick and was silent on his walks except when he passed a neighbor, and then he tipped his hat and said, "Morning," if it were before noon, or, "Evening," if it were after noon, without pausing his walk, just as nowadays joggers will come to a stoplight and continue to jog in place so as not to break their stride. Then the tantrum broke out, blue, without a breath of air. I was an object of time, filled with dread. I lifted the ice cream to make certain no spider was webbed in the cone. Sculpture is the worst possible craft for them to attempt. You could increase the height by making lateral additions and building over them a sequence of steps, leaving tunnels, or windows, between the blocks, and I did. The shape of who's to come. For example, the funny pre-family was constant in its all-purpose itinerant ovals. It should be completed only in the act of being used. While my mother shopped, I stood in *Produce* and ate raw peas. The lovely music of the German violin. Most little children like beer but they outgrow it. Unseen, just heard, hard to remember. My sister was named "after" my aunt, the name not Murree but, like marriage, French, Marie. The first-grade teacher, Miss Sly, was young and she might have been kind, but all the years that she had been named Sly so had made her. A man mitt. I had "hit upon" an idea. Penny, buster. Uneven, and internal, asymmetrical but additive time. A child, meanwhile, had turned her tricycle upside down and was turning the pedal with her hand to make the front wheel spin. The solemn, flickering effects, not knowing what you're doing. In your country do most of the girls do this. A cold but exhibiting hypothesis. I couldn't get the word butterfly so I tried to get the word moth. The man with the pinto pony had come through the neighborhood selling rides for a quarter, or as he said, "two bits," and it was that "two bits" even more than the pony that led the children to believe he was a real cowboy and therefore heroic. He was a trainer of falcons, scornful of hunting dogs. The body is a farmer. From the beginning, they had to drive the plow through stone eggs. She pretends she is making popcorn. The boats appeared to have stopped on the water, moving only as if to breathe. It seemed that they had hardly begun and they were already there. We were sticky in the back seat of the car. In the school bathroom I vomited secretly, not because I was ill but because I so longed for my mother. Now, bid chaos welcome. It requires a committee, all translators. Undone is not not done. And could it be musical if I hate it.

Like plump birds
along the shore

Summers were spent in a fog that rains. They were mirages, no different from those that camelback riders approach in the factual accounts of voyages in which I persistently imagined myself, and those mirages on the highway were for me both impalpable souvenirs and unstable evidence of my own adventures, now slightly less vicarious than before. The person too has flared ears, like an infant's reddened with batting. I had claimed the radio nights for my own. There were more storytellers than there were stories, so that everyone in the family had a version of history and it was impossible to get close to the original, or to know "what really happened." The pair of ancient, stunted apricot trees yielded ancient, stunted apricots. What was the meaning hung from that depend. The sweet aftertaste of artichokes. The lobes of autobiography. Even a minor misadventure, a bumped fender or a newsstand without newspapers, can "ruin the entire day," but a child cries and laughs without rift. The sky droops straight down. I lapse, hypnotized by the flux and reflux of the waves. They had ruined the Danish pastry by frosting it with whipped butter. It was simply a tunnel, a very short one. Now I remember worrying about lockjaw. The cattle were beginning to move across the field pulled by the sun, which proved them to be milk cows. There is so little public beauty. I found myself dependent on a pause, a rose, something on paper. It is a way of saying, I want you, too, to have this experience, so that we are more alike, so that we are closer, bound together, sharing a point of view — so that we are "coming from the same place." It is possible to be homesick in one's own neighborhood. Afraid of the bears. A string of eucalyptus pods was hung by the window to discourage flies. So much of "the way things were" was the same from one day to the next, or from one occasion (Christmas, for example, or July 4th) to the next, that I can speak now of how we "always" had dinner, all of us sitting at our usual places in front of the placemats of woven straw, eating the salad first, with cottage cheese, which my father always referred to as "cottage fromage," that being one of many little jokes with which he expressed his happiness at home. Twice he broke his baby toe, stubbing it at night. As for we who "love to be astonished," my heartbeats shook the bed. In any case, I wanted to be both the farmer and his horse when I was a child, and I tossed my head and stamped with one foot as if I were pawing the ground before a long gallop. Across the school playground, an outing, a field trip, passes in ragged order over the lines which mark the hopscotch patch. It made for a sort of family mythology. The heroes kept clean, chasing dusty rustlers, tonguing the air. They spent the afternoon building a dam across the gutter. There was too much carpeting in the house, but the windows upstairs were left open except on the very coldest or wettest of days. It was there that she met the astonishing figure of herself when young. Are we likely to find ourselves later pondering such suchness amid all the bourgeois memorabilia. Wherever I might find them, however unsuitable, I made them useful by a simple shift. The obvious analogy is with music. Did you mean gutter or guitar. Like cabbage or collage. The book was a sort of protection because it had a better plot. If any can be spared from the garden. They hoped it would rain before somebody parked beside that section of the curb. The fuchsia is a plant much like a person, happy in the out-of-doors in the same sun and breeze that is most comfortable to a person sitting nearby. We had to wash the windows in order to see them. Supper was a different meal from dinner. Small fork-stemmed boats propelled by wooden spoons wound in rubber bands cruised the trough. Losing its balance on the low horizon lay the vanishing vernal day.

Water cannot be a mirror, nor any more like a mirror than the skin of the forehead. The day will twinkle, sparkle, shoot forth its single bits. Breathless through tunnels, breathless past graves. We went down the hill in the afternoons around four when the day had begun to cool under a breeze springing out of the west, which began always at the tops of the poplars and then bent the boughs of the redwood trees, and of which my grandmother always complained, sending one of the grandchildren indoors to her bureau to find her a particular sweater, whose color she would describe, before letting us go downtown for Eskimo Pies, to which I felt we had a special claim, unknown to the man who sold them, because our mother had grown up in Alaska. Still, I had lost the little cluster in which I first saw that yellow spot resembling a blossom or a bee. It's Tubby the Tuba's little melody. A troublemaker who walked in the front door. The catsup that no one tastes because of the shape of the bottle. I was thinking of the slippery love-seat, upholstered in a pattern of roses. Vision determines the view. They are supposed to be offering you a good time, too. She would, if she could. As for we who "love to be astonished," a weasel eats twenty times as much as a lizard of the same size. One is growing up repeatedly. But every night I was afraid that my parents were packing to leave us, so I kept an eye on them. The fence posts were long lozenges covered with moss — ink is darker and wetter than moss — and sunk into gray soil patchy with acrid powdery grass among which grew poison oak and rattlesnake weed. On my mother's side, a matriarchy. I wanted to be a brave child, a girl with guts. And how one goes about educating that would-be audience may very likely determine the history of that moment, its direction, the qualities that become emphatic and characteristic of its later influence.

As if by scratching at the paper one could dig out the names. Things bound in their cases plunge and erupt. Now when I build something, for example, the job does not seem beautifully done until all the tools have been properly put away. Sadness and thirst, and hence sadness and water, have ever since been associated in my imagination. She lay in bed pretending to be a baby or a wounded soldier. The fellow in the dark would be the good guy with a harmonica. He was talking about oil paints, the body of the pigments, and the ground, with its distortions as they're actual, really seen. This is my portrait-bowl. But of any material, the first thing to make is an ashtray. When I wake up in the morning and it's raining, I feel like rolling in the mud. I was eventually to become one person, gathered up maybe, during a pause, at a comma. Roller skating, I could jump lines, hop cracks. What was the meaning hung from that depend but lupine in the pastures, mustard in the vineyards. How was Yosemite. I missed the flavor that chilling had stolen from the peach and the apricot, and the cold of the apple hurt my teeth. The pedal was squeaking on the piano. Can one "feel" that it is an instrument of discontinuity, of consciousness. When the child in my class whom I thought of as my "boyfriend," though we were then only nine years old, was sick and absent from school, I felt concerned, protective, both vulnerable and responsible by virtue of that relationship which was not friendship but love, and I gathered up the homework assignments and his books each day and took them to his house after school. Something is similar. There are various means burrs carry. Others appear to know what they're doing. Tiny explicit pieces of information come out about them that wouldn't have if we'd asked questions. The horse, too, is a farmer. The spasm of a restricted smile, a reflected smile. Like a penalty, the simile. Should they go there they would not find the little village that I knew and loved.

What memory
is not a "gripping"
thought

From here each day seems like a little boat and all the days are swept and tilted back and forth across an immense and distant bay of blue, gray, green. We were like plump birds along the shore, caught by the mortal breaks. Dimension, longevity, color, and pleasure. So that if I tell you my intentions, I force myself to maintain those intentions. I wanted to see a mountain lion but had to content myself with a raccoon. The dog was jealous and pretended to limp. The fog was so fine that it was more like an odor than a texture in the air, an odor of seaweed and roses growing so remarkably red and pink and yellow in that sandy soil. There was something almost religious about it, something idolatrous, something insufficient. That was the break in my sentiments, resembling waves, which I might have longed to recover. I think they were cicadas, though off the trees. Behind the freeway we passed a shop selling "antiques" and "collectables." The child gawks, the child is gawky. She hated us to ask what's for dinner, since the planning and recitation of the menu bored her, though the thought of cooking it didn't, and all she replied was, "Decisions, decisions." She asked for "something with my coffee sweet." My grandfather had two horses, old Duke, "a fine animal," and High Spot, with his rider, cantering in place, so that sitting on his back was like sitting pretty. Continuity, not so much of ideas as of assumptions, or attitudes, a style one simply can't break away from. We returned slowly back up the hill, walking backwards at the steepest part, as if to fool our legs, and yet, during another later summer, when I worked as a hiking instructor at a girls' camp in New England, I discovered that the downhill walk, at least after a full day of climbing in the mountains, can be the most painful part of the hike, one's legs giving way, the constant trembling in their muscles causing the girls behind me (for

I always went in front, and in fact was racing always away from the girls, urgent with alienation and anxious to be alone, since I hated the camp and was persistently homesick) to giggle. We see a land of rolling hills, beginning that summer. How would your day-by-day record of weather go. The pants pockets are close to the body, keeping the pennies warm. Or haylike, and muzzy. As for we who "love to be astonished," I'm not your maid I'm your mother. Little sailboats were capsizing in the bay. It didn't seem the least bit amazing that they had tunneled the highway through the living redwood tree, for in so doing they had changed the tree into the tunnel, made it something it had not been before, and separated it forever from any other tree. The universal is animated by individuality. A name trimmed with colored ribbons. Shaped by the world since seventeen-five-forty-one. They sing funny little numbers all praising the numerous pleasures. They insisted on the importance, the primacy, of "inner resources" and "inner qualities of mind," so that one could "bear up" under any circumstances. An old building creaks, more so by water. A force of penmanship. There are places in it that I never revisited. Five or six children in the neighborhood were playing on the front porch, pretending to be pirates and shouting at cars on the street to "stand to" and "drop sail." She cultivated a particular garden, the rose garden (or rose bed), the azalea garden, the garden of indigenous plants (oddly, less opulent than the others). Little children should ride on the backs of old horses, not on ponies. If we didn't have to eat we'd be rich, I said, imitating something to say. I had marveled at the immense difference between the animals at the zoo and the gulls, pigeons, sparrows, and starlings that were only visitors there. There is even a dominant finch. Collaborate with the occasion. The obvious analogy is with music. Their activities, being more natural, since they were doing what they "did" in their own milieu (while we stood around the enclosure waiting and hoping that the sleeping tigers would "do" something soon), should in fact have interested us more. Our dog will eat broccoli. Mischief logic; Miss Chief. I would be aloof, dark, indirect, and upsetting or I would be a center of patience and material calm. So that later, playing alone, I could imagine myself developing into a tree, and then I yearned to do so with so much desire that it made me shapeless, restless, sleepless, demanding, disagreeable.

We have come
a long way from what
we actually felt

If it were writing we would have to explain. I say that as much to comfort myself as to state something I think to be true. Dashing up out of the dark basement, pursued by the humid fear. Similarly, due to some peculiar sentimentality, people always want the runt of the litter. She sat every afternoon in her chair waiting for her headache, exactly as one might sit on a bench awaiting a bus. In a book I read the sentence, "the water is as blue as ink," which made me regret that so few people use fountain pens. Never give the blindman money without taking one of his pencils. When I went to Christian Science Sunday school, the teacher asked me what I wanted to be when I grew up, and I answered that I wanted to be a writer or a doctor. The words of the last one to speak continued to hover in the air, and that was embarrassing. A name trimmed with colored ribbons. At the circus men were selling live chameleons which wore tiny collars and were attached to red and yellow ribbons that one could pin to one's dress or shirt as a living jewel. As for we who "love to be astonished," mother love. The game of solitaire, of patience, is disappointing when it "comes out" the first time. It is impossible to return to the state of mind in which these sentences originated. So I borrowed my father's typewriter. There was a garden, a hole in the fence, a grandfather who had no religion—one can run through the holes in memory, wearing a wet hat, onto the sidewalk covered with puddles, and there are fingers in them. Similarly, a beautiful concert or an unusual autumn sunset makes me feel restless if I'm by myself, wanting someone with whom to share it. At noon, under no one's new moon. I didn't want the kids over to play, messing with my stuff. We were coughing after a day by the sea. That was the gap between behavior and feeling. This was a year at the breaking point, turning over, given the swift combination. That summer when I was nine I trained myself to hold my breath and stubbornly swim the full length of the pool underwater and back, until the returning end of the pool went black. In the telephone room one heard the disembodied voice over the receiver while staring into the row of empty coats and hats, and when we played hide and seek with the other cousins, on those occasions when my grandparents had all the family to dinner, only the oldest cousins dared hide among them. An other is a possibility, isn't it. I have been spoiled with privacy, permitted the luxury of solitude. A pause, a rose, something on paper. I didn't want a party for my tenth birthday, I wanted my mother, who was there, of course, at the party, but from whom I was separated by my friends and because she was busy with the cake and the balloons. She kept a diary but she never read it. Yet those who scorn friendship can, without illusion but not without some remorse, be the finest friends in the world. Now the shower curtain is sexy. The gap indicated that objects or events had been forgotten, that a place was being held for them, should they chance to reappear. The sound of the truck had frightened the towhees away. Like the "big, round O" taught by the traditional penmanship teachers (the Palmer method, it was called), there was a big round "A" and we were to pronounce it, in place of the nasty, narrow, nasal "A" in words like cat and Ann. The high curb turned on the curve. The windows on the northwestern wall looked out toward the clock on the so-called Campanile by which my father, far-sighted, kept time. What was the meaning hung from that depend. Apples have bellies. She was a skinny little girl and her bathing suit fit her so loosely that when she sat to play on the beach the sand fell into the crotch and filled it like a little pouch. The toll bridge takes its toll, the span its fog, its paint. Nevertheless fleas, and therefore powders. You are not different from your friend, but with your friend you are different from yourself, and recognizing that,

I withdrew, wanting to protect my honesty, because I had defined integrity on two dimensions. I pushed my thumb to make a lever of the blunt spoon, he took up the palette knife and ships came out of the blue, I hit the space bar. Actually I don't remember whether my father went with Braque or was only invited to do so one fine day outside of Paris to paint a landscape in plain air. And finally, on a visit to the zoo, as we were passing by the enclosure where the silver foxes were kept, I saw a flock of sparrows pecking at the ground of the enclosure, and one of them, venturing too close to a fox which was crouching in the shadow of an artificial rock, was suddenly seized by the fox, who swallowed it in a moment.

It is hard to turn away
from moving water

A point, in motion, is a line. I wouldn't look up. Every child wanted to be blackboard monitor in order to clap the chalk erasers at the end of the day. But a squirrel had come down the chimney and was trapped in the living room, and there, in its panic, it had run over the shelves, knocking the knickknacks to the floor. On a building of fake brickwork people were pausing for a break way up where I would be nauseous. It being impossible to complete the thought, the idea of infinity or eternity elicited a sort of desire, the sexual side of thought. Wild horses couldn't keep. The Chinese woman in the laundromat spoke, and her tiny steps were out of keeping with the raucous voice, sped up. Like a mermaid blowing a fog tuba. Aesthetic discoveries are socially different from scientific discoveries, and this difference is political. I began to clean my desk by dumping everything onto the bed and wiping the drawers with a washcloth. That third phrase of "Earth Angel" was difficult. Over and over again we took pet cocoons captive, but I never saw a single moth or butterfly emerge. He spoke loudly, as though in order to be heard above the silence of a library. There was a different colored toothbrush for each member of the family. Americans say "janitor" rather than "custodian." It is a name trimmed with colored ribbons. Polish tinfoil with pennies and make silver. Should he chance to say what he was doing, he would disguise the saying so as to throw one off the track, describing, for example, a passenger on a plane while neglecting to tell us where the plane was headed, or narrating a dream of the night before when asked what he had been doing recently. The voice in the dark doorway blocks the image. Meanwhile, I was growing up as a cowgirl, a child doctor, a great reader. This rigorous inclusion must eventually turn over on itself. Where I refer to "a preliminary" I mean that until 1964 I regarded the world as a medium of recognition and I prepared for it to recognize me. A person does not look the same in a mirror as she does. Swollen glands, sore throat, headache, slight fever—all some kind of mistake. Organizing a lot of material into a general view. That was the most interesting thing I have ever seen at a zoo. A fuchsia becomes exhausted in a heavy wind. My aunt, holding up the little letter I had written, insisted that the act of writing-down was testimonial and that the writing would always be used as proof of what I held to be true. She, too, was a clumsy athlete. As for we who "love to be astonished," every Sears smells the same. I stopped eating corn on the cob and lobster, not because I no longer liked the taste but because I disliked the mess. A cluttered room makes for a cluttered mind. We had captured dozens of polliwogs in paper cups and they were swimming in the bathroom sink while I tried to fill a small fishbowl with clean water, but the bowl didn't quite fit under the faucet and in trying to make it fit I accidentally knocked the plug aside, so that all the water, carrying all the polliwogs, drained away while I watched. What memory is not a "gripping" thought. The mind was stocked. It was only in the summers that we were allowed to buy comic books, and then only once a week and with our own money. Queasy innards. There might be some sort of thematic connection between the man you were and the monkey you become. If I couldn't be a cowboy, then I wanted to be a sailor. What was the meaning hung from that depend. Today the clouds appear to be entering the world from one spot in the sky. If ideas are like air, you can't steal them. Proves porous, held in. This morning I am enchanted by its grace.

I wrote my name in　　It was awhile before I understood what
every one of his books　　had come between the stars, to form the
constellations. They were at a restaurant
owned by Danes. Now that I was "old
enough to make my own decisions," I
dressed like everyone else. People must
flatter their own eyes with their pathetic
lives. The things I was saying followed logically the things that I
had said before, yet they bore no relation to what I was thinking
and feeling. There was once a crooked man, who rode a crooked
mile—thereafter he wrote in a crooked style characteristic of nine-
teenth-century prose, a prose of science with cumulative sentences.
The ideal was of American property and she had received it from a
farmer. It includes buying thrillers and gunmen's coats. I was more
terrified of the FBI agents than of the unspecified man who had
kidnapped, murdered, and buried the girl in the other fifth grade,
in the hill behind school. A pause, a rose, something on paper. It
was at about this time that my father provided me with every right
phrase about the beauty and wonder of books. Colored cattle were
grazing on a California hillside, so much of a single yellow that from
this distance and at this hour it was impossible to see any gradation
of light and shadow. Individuality is animated by its sense of the
infinite. I play a sentimental role. The debater "makes his point,"
and in games, points tell the winner. These one suddenly finds child-
ish, embarrassing, but not yet dull. Fallow power, bright red and
yellow. We say thought wanders where it should sweep. As for we
who "love to be astonished," she pretends she is a blacksmith. In
the hot lot beside the tire dealer a crew of two eats lunch. There is
always plenty to do until one is bored, and then the boredom itself
generates the lack, generates its own necessary conditions. The su-
28)　pernatural makes it cry. Now she's a violinist. What is certain, at

least, is that one must avoid dishonest work. I quote my mother's mother's mother's mother's mother: "I must every day correct some fault in my morality and talents and remember how short a time I have to live." You might say she created her reality simply because she "would not have it, any other way." It is hard to turn away from moving water. She suggested we take "a nice nap." Even when I was too old for the pony rides at the park, I loved the little creatures, and I watched my younger sister clinging to the saddle horn as the ponies plodded around the narrow circle, feeling superior, since on Saturdays I took riding lessons on real horses, and yet envious, too, since it was not Saturday and it was my sister and not I who was riding now. You are so generous, they told me, allowing everything its place, but what we wanted to hear was a story. A blare of sound, a roar of life, a vast array of human hives, reveling in education. What a situation. Whenever you've exhausted setting, topic, or tone, begin a new paragraph. The refrigerator makes a sound I can't spell. The finches have come at last to the feeder. The magician had come to entertain the children at the birthday party. It was called mush, and we ate it for breakfast in patterns, like pudding. We were like plump birds along the shore. Green night divining trees, scooped too. What memory is not a "gripping" thought. But it's a happy song. It took all day. He had stolen a tin of nuts and given them to me and now I had to return them to the store, like a thief returning to the shelf, but I managed to pull it off and put them back. The romance of the vanished. I had begun to learn, from the experience of passionate generosity, about love.

Religion is
a vague lowing

Learning to listen, that is taught not to talk. Can one take captive the roar of the city. Simon says sounds from the schoolyard. If I'm standing here then I must be positive. We are taking from the neighbor's rain, which goes damp and tight around my waist. Obey the best. We were like plump birds, then, walking stiffly in a sandy wind along the shore. Foxtails, the juice of a peach, have fallen on the flesh of this book. The secret of the song was that one couldn't hum it; the melody was elusive, or not apparent at all. Women, I heard, should speak softly without mumbling. The obvious analogy is with music. Perhaps alienation was privilege. I was bored at the ballgame, afraid of the ball. Then out of burlap I made saddlebags. We raked the piled leaves onto an old sheet, tied the corners, and carried the bundle over to the fall fire. One can discover the name of one's true love by plucking daisy petals, jumping rope, or counting the tiny white spots of imperfection on a fingernail. I felt self-sufficient except with regard to my feelings, to which I was always vulnerable, always in relation to someone else. We pay attention to other things. A white but warmer winter, the weather better now when she is old enough for the Botanical Gardens, the Bird Refuge. Music with its supply of notes, one of them going up (rising). A stranger's eye would naturally move. The world seen in a foreign English, as awkward as surprising, with a vocabulary from the thesaurus instead of from the dictionary. I may have started inexactly, I thought, nearsighted to a buttercup; I will begin again, and I rolled over into the next indentation. A name trimmed with colored ribbons. The glass fixture in the kitchen was covered with grease and tiny black flies that had died in it. One enjoys the summer evening until the mosquitoes come out, pursued by bats. As for we who "love to be astonished," a moth has more flesh than a butterfly could lift. From the bus I saw the blind woman, whose seeing-eye dog sleeps on her sweater while she sells tissue-paper carnations on Geary Street. Lizards get their prey. They resemble, with their bluish hours, the local light. From the window I could see the July Fourth fireworks and the winter rains fall into the bay. It was not so much monotony as a certain obsession with thought. Old, satisfying corners, I made to stop, they made to move. The swan is a bitch. She was so at ease that her bad manners were graceful. Who'd made warmer ways, a kid knows more. He should have given us a "hard right" instead of an "easy left." They were not then, as in these days, interchangeable terms. Math is like a joke I just don't get, whose punchline isn't funny. It would be pleasant to wait, if possible. But the margin is not "purer." Adolescence is repetitious, moment by moment beginnings in the middle. I wrote my name in blue ink on the first page of every one of his books. That old horse Duke has a gentle trot, was sentimental, fast. Poor ducks in this cold.

Any photographer
will tell you the same

Somewhere during the transition from childhood to womanhood, a girl is likely to become interested in religion. It would be appropriate to call this not intuition but pre-knowing, or paranoia. They asked my mother to correct my views or to keep me home. Blindmen sell brooms. From hypochondria come sentences and memory. In California during the summer the shadows are very dark and cool, the sunlight hot and bright. But, because we have only seven days, the light seems to be orderly, even predictable. A pause, a rose, something on paper implicit in the fragmentary text. The Mayan calendar has more days. The plump but uncertain girl grew righteous with love of the puce horizon. It is hard to turn away from moving water. Often gruff and bellowing, always female, but not always feminine. I imagined the pre-absence that occurs before one is born and thought that that was god. Preparation. I would not allow myself to fall asleep during the long drive to the country until we had passed through the town of Alviso, where the migrant workers lived, so that I could see the rows of outhouses that lined the edge of the fields. The squirrel had knocked over the Dresden figurine, where my grandmother came from. We can "plan the weekend." As for we who "love to be astonished," you would say these are its ghosts. In New England, the weather builds character. I discovered that I could never quite remember how my favorite songs went. Irritated by motorbikes. After a certain point, one no longer hears any new ideas, must make do with new facts. The dance is best seen from the upper balcony. Take your place (one) not your places. He framed his sentences carefully. The sunrise falls through the windows. At home, in my reveries, with the split line on my palm to show a real life. It can hardly be subdivided. A standing, a leaving, an opening. Constellations, with stars, are nothing absorbed by a place. It might seem as if philosophy had been taken over by artists. The screen can be taken away from the fire as long as someone is sitting in the room. The horses in the dewy field overlope. What should I adjust but remorse and voluntary perception (for which I kept a notebook), just as a responsible person with a new watch absorbs the lateness of a friend. But I don't like horse races because you don't get a chance to see the horses. The fox that survives is successful. It was winter but a warm night in New England for taking a walk in the snow crunch. Bleach had killed the mildew. What is one doing to, or with, the statement (the language) or the stated (the object or the idea) when one *means* it. A bottle of wine is different from a wine bottle. And milk in the warm snow delivered by a milkman. She worried that the wheel might come off at sixty-five. There are always more leaves than flowers. In the breeze they occupy the eyes with the wobble of the rough circles of a self. I, with crashing consequity, waited, wanting to have experienced many, many things.

At the time the
perpetual Latin of love
kept things hidden

Was she taking herself seriously or taking herself too seriously. Take as straight lines the chords of the bounding circle. Dark parties. One would not read the book unless one already understood it. Running with a herd of deer, then feeling scattered. No matter where we go out for our walk, we always end up by the creek. We cut through the cornfield, each of us eating two or three ears of corn snatched from the stalk, marveling at the fools who didn't know that raw corn tastes so much sweeter than cooked. We would have been kicked away if we'd been cats. They played marbles with sow bugs, stepped on snails, watched the slugs froth under a sprinkling of salt—small vertical cruelties in a benevolent climate. I smell the smell of adhesive tape, of wounds. Language which is like a fruitskin around fruit. The zebras were not at all like horses and could not serve as a substitute in this tale of Africa. Any photographer will tell you the same. Hence, lacking, not in authenticity, but in reality. Why should these people be writing to each other. It's true that there are times when it is embarrassing to have come from California. The late afternoon light, which my mother always referred to as "backlighting," gentled the greens, with blue and gray. I only want the facts. It's okay to have pancakes for dinner. Before a busy day, one wants to "get" a lot of sleep. A pause, a rose, something on paper. She wanted to stand aside, keep to herself, remain quiet, but too frequently something in her nature presented a conflict, a confusion, a sound. Wanting to "explain" is like having a memory—the person posits itself elsewhere, adolescent-like, as a figure in the distance escaping, while awaiting the advent of its more glorious self but modestly, even piously. Faces return with menace to the window. They lack an appetite. The car sat, a saddled pelican, hood up. Restlessness is a form of doubt as well as a form of curiosity. As for we who "love to be astonished," he's a walker. My grandmother had been a Christian Scientist, but somehow I turned the teachings, emphasizing not the perfectibility of the body but the power of the mind to corrupt it, so that I became a hypochondriac and worried about turning insane. A name trimmed with colored ribbons. A natural morphine at the scene of an accident. A person feels remorse for individualism and about beauty. That is something that I learned and it seems to apply to everything, at least as a way of making or caring for things. The inevitable sentiment is a preliminary. He had stopped eating cheese in order to lose weight. Each side of Jack's box was painted like a half domino, which is a die, in bright colors. Were you friends with this man. I wrote my name in every one of his books. Was my little handwriting dainty, or afraid. It was a pretty plaything. She trimmed first her nails and then the split ends of her hair. Considering the immediate, considering the same, small. All many details needed for seeing, they are like a walking stick. Spin it, then weave it, and wear it out, out. The synchronous keeps its reversible logic, and in this it resembles psychology, or the logic of a person.

She showed the left profile, the good one

A man is tall, a mountain is high, the sky's the limit. The spare was flat. The filled valleys made shorter hills which we crested on snowshoes on snow over fences. It seemed that we had hardly begun and we were already there. Personal, oblige, running down. At the time, I saw my life as a struggle against my fate, that is, my personality. She was trapped in the elevator panting in plenty of air. Wounded by gossip's rat-a-tattle. More than horse work on worse hills. On a scroll in the case the sequence of plump wrestlers resembled stages in the development of the blooms on the snapdragons. They were driven indoors by the bees. Each time we entered the Metro in Paris I read the small sign which reserved the large facing double seats nearest the door for soldiers and veterans crippled by war, and it was just that small sign that realized for me the place-name and its history. Writing maybe held it, separated, there to see. When you open a letter do you hope for a check. A pause, a rose, something on paper. Duck eggs taste "eggier." One form of shyness is characterized by the fear of making someone else feel awkward or embarrassed, a kind of heightened sensitivity or extreme empathy. Religion is a vague lowing. I often felt "jittery" and took long walks, trying to get a long way from what I actually felt. Ring, plunge, reappear. Bucephalus, Traveler, creatures carrying history. Just off shore she saw seven whales, and then ten, leaping from the water and rolling into it again. As for we who "love to be astonished," so do all relationships move. You have to take on the role of pack leader with your dog. Roaring downtown, the lights ahead out of the blue. A tiny red rocking horse, a plaything, bright and sweet. Any photographer will tell you the same. We took along a loaf of Wonder Bread for the ducks. I have learned to be suspicious of those sudden and spontaneous acts of generosity, for it was in such a mood that I gave away the little wicker rocking chair which had been mine throughout my childhood and had belonged to my mother before that, immediately regretting the gesture, so much so that I couldn't bring myself to ask for its return, since I couldn't do so casually and without resentment, a resentment for which I felt guilty, selfish, embarrassed. There is no greater temptation than that of reminiscence. What memory is not a "gripping" thought. She was born with that stubborn temperament, and it has shaped the particular seriousness by virtue of which she has carried out her intentions. A spiral is the shape of a progression of circles. Thus myopia may serve to dispel the pains of chronophobia. The obvious analogy is with music. Thought it through and through. The inaccessibility of the meaning intrigued me all the more, since I couldn't read the single letters, if that is what they were, the little marks which constitute Persian. Mother dimension; sex. She observed that detail minutely, as if it were botanical. As if words could unite an ardent intellect with the external material world. Listen to the drips. The limits of personality. It's in the nature of language to encourage, and in part to justify, such Faustian longings. Break them up into uncounted continuous and voluminous digressions. The very word "diary" depresses me.

The tree rows in orchards are capable of patterns. What were Caesar's battles but Caesar's prose. A name trimmed with colored ribbons. We "took" a trip as if that were part of the baggage we carried. In other words, we "took our time." The experience of a great passion, a great love, would remove me, elevate me, enable me at last to be both special and ignorant of the other people around me, so that I would be free at last from the necessity of appealing to them, responding to them. That is, to be nearly useless but at rest. There were cut flowers in vases and some arrangements of artificial flowers and ceramic bouquets, but in those days they did not keep any living houseplants. The old fragmentary texts, early Egyptian and Persian writings, say, or the works of Sappho, were intriguing and lovely, a mystery adhering to the lost lines. At the time, the perpetual Latin of love kept things hidden. It was not his fate to be as famous as Segovia. Nonetheless, I wrote my name in every one of his books. Language is the history that gave me shape and hypochondria. And followed it with a date, as if by my name I took the book and by the date, historically, contextualized its contents, affixed to them a reading. And memory a wall. My grandmother had been a great beauty and she always won at cards. As for we who "love to be astonished," the ear is less active than the eye. The artichoke has done its best, armored, with scales, barbed, and hiding in its interior the soft hairs so aptly called the choke. I suppose I had always hoped that, through an act of will and the effort of practice, I might be someone else, might alter my personality and even my appearance, that I might in fact create myself, but instead I found myself trapped in the very character which made such a thought possible and such a wish mine. Any work dealing with questions of possibility must lead to new work. In between pieces, they shuffled their feet. The white legs of the pear trees, protected from the sun. Imagine, please: morbid myopia. The puppy is perplexed by the lizard which moves but has no smell. We were like plump birds along the shore, unable to run from the water. Could there be swans in the swamp. Of course, one continues to write, and thus to "be a writer," because one has not yet written that "ultimate" work. Exercise will do it. I insert a description: of agonizing spring morning freshness, when through the open window a smell of cold dust and buds of broken early grass, of schoolbooks and rotting apples, trails the distant sound of an airplane and a flock of crows. I thought that for a woman health and comfort must come after love. Any photographer will tell you the same. So I wouldn't wear boots in the snow, nor socks in the cold. Shufflers scuff. That sense of responsibility was merely the context of the search for a lover, or, rather, for a love. Let someone from the other lane in. Each boat leaned toward us as it turned and we, pretending to know more than we did, identified each class as it was blown by. Politics get wider as one gets older. I was learning a certain geometry of purely decorative shapes. One could base a model for form on a crystal or the lungs. She showed the left profile, the good one. What she felt, she had heard as a girl. The point of the foghorns is that you can't see them, need to hear them. More by hive than by heart the mathematics of drones makes it noticeable. It was May, 1958, and reading was anti-anonymous. She disapproved of background music.

It flies in the night. In that light it is obvious that you are related to your mother. Boots, plows, cheese, burls. As for we who "love to be astonished," the night is lit. Remarkably to learn to look. My father would say I've a "big day" tomorrow. Words are not always adequate to the occasion, and my "probably" sounded hopeless. It's real, why, so, it's wrong. I mentioned my face because I am made that way wonderfully like a shadow I do not despise. But if I don't like the first dress I try on, I won't like any. It is only a coincidence. Whose shadow who's. At the circus the elephants were more beautiful than the horses, more touching than the clowns, and more graceful than the tigers trained to jump on their backs. Physical education was required. At school, the choral director described the torso in terms of the muscles of sound. Always infinity extends from any individual life, but eternity is limited between one's birth and one's death. Interpreting such combinations of events, and the sort of mysticism on which such interpretations are based, is what gives coincidence its bad name. Religion is a vague lowing. I was beginning to look for some meaning when I should have been satisfied with events. It is hard to turn away from moving water. For the time, being; twilight seen even full. I mean to say "hopelessly" in a promising tone, as one would say, "hopelessly in love," and mean, really, "very much," and, especially, "full of hope." In my "trouble with conflict," I was reluctant to be disconcerting, to cause discontinuity. Panic versus crystallographic form. Knickknacks are for browsers. There is some discomfort more active than boredom but none more fatiguing. I had gone back to bed and was pretending to sleep in order to avoid saying goodbye to the friends who had been visiting, hiding from farewell's display. The lives of which I read seemed more real than my own, but I still seemed more real than the persons who had led them. A sunlit winter's day lay thin, frozen to the hummocks and rubble of mud in the cold but erotic marshlands beside the Concord River. We have come a long way from what we actually felt. But he remains aloof, saying only that things *seem* familiar. The invisible but realistic detail of an ultimate monument. By hand, put together, with hook and thread. Poco Bueno was buried, saddled, standing. To do things for the sake of fame or other gain is selfish, but to do them for your own pleasure is to do them generously. One might become a volunteer down with the poor Italians. At least, we shall solve the riddle presented by money, or so he says. It seemed that we had hardly begun and we were already there. Memory is the money of my class. What a vast! what a business! The lowly cabbage strives and the turnip in the garden yearns to be a person. You know, things like that. Systems betray, or are, as in a "made place," made betrayals. I was organized by addition and addiction. I found a penny in a calla lily.

Such displacements
alter illusions, which is
all-to-the-good

Those birds are saying, over and over, this tree, my branch, my field of seeds, my herd of worms. Thus was it told to me. I made signs to them to be as quiet as possible. It was at this time, I think, that I became interested in science. Is that a basis for descriptive sincerity. I am a shard, signifying isolation — here I am thinking aloud of my affinity for the separate fragment taken under scrutiny. Yet that was only a coincidence. The penny disk, the rarer dollar disk. Her hair is the color of a brass bedstead. We were proud of our expertise, distinguishing the ripe ears of corn from the green, speaking knowledgeably of tassels and the breeds of corn: Butter & Sugar, Country Gentleman, Honey & Cream, Silver Queen. The old dirt road, broken into clods and gullies, or clods and ruts, over which I was walking under some noisy trees, had been reversed in the dark. And so I was returning. For such words present residences on a brown ground. A pause, a rose, something on paper. When I was a child, the mailman, Tommy, let us walk his route with him until we reached the busy streets, and then he sent us home, dragging the dog. The sky was studied with stars, he said, white, low, as heavy as stones. It was utterly sincere, though not completely sincere. That troubled my reply. I wasn't guiding, I was fleeing the little charges, campers over whom I was counselor, whom I left resting, while I in a frenzy of self-absorption raced for solitude. On such a hot day, a "scorcher," the wind helps. An airplane passes over the baseball game and one hears it in the air and over the air, amplified by the transistor radios belonging to the fans. Stay, after the others go. It convinced a few and attracted many. Live birds are heavier than air. She showed the left profile, the good one, with the light behind her casting a shadow on the near side of her face. Any photographer will tell you the same. I am looking for the little hand mirror. The summer evenings saw window shoppers in a reflecting system, man with merchandise agog. It is hard to turn away from moving water. All summer I worked as a mountain guide and behind me hiked a group of girls giggling in descent of a president. He made me nervous as soon as he began offering a special discount. But the work is probably a good deal wiser than the horny old doctor he was. I wrote my name in every one of his books. A name trimmed with colored ribbons. They used to be the leaders of the avant-garde, but now they just want to be understood, and so farewell to them. If I was left unmarried after college, I would be single all my life and lonely in old age. In such a situation it is necessary to make a choice between contempt and an attempt at understanding, and yet it is difficult to know which is the form of retreat. We will only understand what we have already understood. The turkey is a stupid bird. And it is scanty praise to be so-called well-meaning. But is there an independent quality, a self-sufficient quality, that is pleasure, and is it comparable to red, fame, and wealth or to beauty (one can feel some affinity for the several distinct categories). Mouth with a radical math claps. The wash lines run with garments hung. A leaf is shed from the potted fuchsia falling in a forest. Enormous boulders perpetually gliding upward.

The coffee drinkers
answered ecstatically

The traffic drones, where drones is a noun. Whereas the cheerful pessimist suits herself in a bad world, which is however the inevitable world, impossible of improvement. I close one eye, always the left, when looking out onto the glare of the street. What education finally serves us, if at all. There is a pause, a rose, something on paper. The small green shadows make the red jump out. That is not a telescope, nor do I have stars in my belly. Such displacements alter illusions, which is all-to-the-good. Now cars not cows wander on the brown hills, and a stasis of mobile homes grows on roads which have taken their names from what grew in the valleys near Santa Clara. We have all grown up with it. If it is personal, it is most likely fickle. The university was the cultural market but on Sundays she tried out different churches. In the museum, attention shifted from painting to painting, the eye forced around, so that it was impossible to focus on any single work. The nightmare was of a giant bluebottle fly which buzzed, "I'm all there is." Where cars don't go are shortcuts. My grandfather was forced to recognize his age when another, younger, man offered his seat on the bus. When one travels, one might "hit" a storm. The shoe must be tied to the ankle. As for we who "love to be astonished," McDonald's is the world's largest purchaser of beef eyeballs. They went out with bows and armbands to shoot at the hay. It's as easy as waves, slopping water. Traverse, watch, and cease. He had the hands of an artist. Penelope reworking the twill. Europeans shake hands more often than we do, here in America, yet I don't think that constitutes a "daring to touch." I'll just keep myself from picking up the telephone, in order to get some work done. What memory is not a "gripping" thought. Only fragments are accurate. Break it up into single words, charge them to combination. So we go into the store shopping and get, after awhile, you know, contralto! Thinking about time in the book, it is really the time of your life. I was experiencing love, immensely relieved. It was, I know, an unparticular spirit of romance. She apologizes and seizes us in the grip of her inadequacies. Giving the back-up okay to the loaded semi. It was a long, three-story apartment building with the apartments set like drawers into slots, and windows only at the front and back. I wouldn't mind if we were actually paying for something with our tax dollars. She threw off her coat, took off her dress. It was not difficult to interpret her mother's clatter at the sink, sometimes the voice of comfort, sometimes the voice of reprimand. You must water the ivy that is creeping up to the bird bell. The morning is past and the sun remains but the sunlight is brighter. The study of painting is exhausting and the sea always gets larger—here I quote Tintoretto. Twigs are the many sounds of light. Could the prairie be this sea—for love. What I felt was that figs resemble kidneys.

We are not forgetting the patience of the mad, their love of detail

The summer countryside, with the round hills patchy and dry, reminding one of a yellow mongrel dog, was what one could call a dirty landscape, the hills colored by the dusty bare ground rather than by grass, and yet this is what seemed like real country to me. I had idealized the pioneer's life, sinking roots. Known for its fleas. One could touch the flesh of their secrets, the roses of their behavior. A) Survey the whole B) lawn and note C) how near shadows D) increase the light. One didn't know what to give a young woman. Watermen are such as row in boats. They don't hear a word of all this, floating like plump birds along the shore. In extending, then entangling their concerns, they are given a thousand new names. The lace-curtain Irish hate neighborhood Blacks. The coffee drinkers answered ecstatically. We looked at the apartment and took it. Space, has small neighborhoods. Idea 13.779: the same insanity of the invariable person. As for we who "love to be astonished," each new bit of knowledge is merely indicative of a wider ignorance. There are ecstasies of rock and of vacuum. One might cultivate a charming defect, say a romantic limp or a little squint. Reluctance. I made curtains out of colored burlap from Sears, hung them at the four windows of the green apartment. A few months earlier I had taken a creative writing class, and now I was painting on three-by-three canvases, on which with several intersecting continuous lines I drew the head with hair, neck, shoulders, face, and hat but without shading, and I filled in the discrete spaces with separate tones from a carefully limited palette. There was threnodious roaring in the year, and I knew it was Freudian. Down manholes, through pipes, to the mysterious sea. Though the pantry smelled more strongly of spices than of herbs and was dominated by nutmeg, the kitchen itself tended to smell of everything that had ever been cooked, but only because it was dark. It formed a dense compact with boulders. If you cut your fingernails they will grow back thick, blunt, like a man's. In a little while, he said, we should be thumbing home. There were five little kittens under the car. They had put curves in the highway to keep drivers awake. The obvious analogy is with music, which extends beyond the space the figure occupies. She was pumping her violin over the piano. Each evening before dinner my parents sat for awhile in the "study," to talk, while my mother knit decoratively designed French sweaters called Jacquard. The house sparrow is a weaver finch. The front door key is hidden under the aloe. How did the artist think to put that on the outside. Such displacements alter illusions, which is all-to-the-good. Now I too could find a perfect cantaloupe, not by poking at the flesh around the stem of the melon but by sniffing at it. At some point hunger becomes sensuous, then lascivious. Not a fuck but a hug. My mother threw away all those little objects of sentiment, billed foolishness. The reference is a distraction, a name trimmed with colored ribbons. It was Father's Day, a holiday that no one could take seriously, yet someone admitted that he was planning to telephone his parents that evening and another said she might do the same. What can those birds be saying. That day there was wind but no air, because we were inland. Then cataloguing the travel books in the library I got the mania for panorama which predicts the desire for accurate representation. Is pink pretty.

Reason looks
for two, then arranges
it from there

Where I woke and was awake, in the room fitting the wall, withdrawn, I had my desk and thus my corner. While waiting, waltz. The soles of our boots wear thin, but the soles of our feet grow thick. The difference between "he presented his argument" and "they had an argument." I still respond to the academic year, the sound of the school bell, the hot Wednesday morning after Labor Day. Must the physiologist stand apart from the philosopher. We are not forgetting the patience of the mad, their love of detail. The sudden brief early morning breeze, the first indication of a day's palpability, stays high in the trees, while flashing silver and green the leaves flutter, a bird sweeps from one branch to another, the indistinct shadows lift off the crumpled weeds, smoke rises from the gravel quarry—all this is metonymy. The "argument" is the plot, proved by the book. Going forward and coming back later. Even posterity, alas, will know Sears. As for we who "love to be astonished," there are fences keeping cyclones. Might be covered, on the ground, by no distance. She spread her fingers as she spoke, talking of artifice, which extends beauty beyond nature. Perhaps it is only a coincidence. For, as Nietzsche put it, "If a man has character, he will have the same experience over and over again." In the morning at eight I sense the first threat of monotony. Give a penny with a knife. Candor is the high pitch of scrutiny. I was tired of ideas, or, rather, the activity of ideas, a kind of exercise, had first invigorated me and then made me sleepy, so that I felt just as one does after a long, early morning walk, returning unable to decide whether to drink more coffee or go back to sleep. The uncommon run of keeping oneself to oneself. The piggy-back plant is okay. Tell anyone who telephones that I'm not home. I liked doing that, had made rooms for dolls on trucks that way, looking in on them through windows. It was a pretense of keeping our distance from anything that appeared pretentious. A sorry mess, but well-framed. As if a contorted checkerboard formed the portrait of a handsome woman in a hat of several ochers and umbers. The dog circles more than a moth before resting. Let the traffic pass. They were on vacation and therefore bored. Someone wanted to go away from everywhere forever but jumped into the bay. We were warned such accidents happen while mothers talk on phones. A doodled gnarled tree. Milk belongs to the mythology of cats but it makes them sick. Ours was a stray with ringworm. One night each year on Boston's Beacon Hill the curtains remained undrawn and the public was invited to peek in. I didn't wear my dark glasses because I didn't want a raccoon tan. Yet this needs shading in. It seemed that I didn't, after all, want a birthday empty of sentimentality. It's on the compulsive buyer's rack up front. The real adversary of my determination was determinism, regulating and limiting the range and degree of difference between things of one day and things of the next. I got it from Darwin, Freud, and Marx. Not fragments but metonymy. Duration. Language makes tracks.

I never swept the sand from where I was going to sit down

It isn't a small world, but there are many ways of dividing it into small parts. Reason looks for two, then arranges it from there. I used as many ideas to become intellectually concentric. The flower for the bee, the berry for the bird. Rainy flower fireworks. It may present the illusion that present experience is familiar. As it were. We have to keep up the good work in order to keep up the good mood. My parents complained that the narrow upstairs hallway was a waste of space, where the worn rose carpet passed between four windows on the one wall and two rooms on the other, made a wish they hadn't moved. Imagine a field before harvest, or better. As for we who "love to be astonished," life is linked to man. Religion is a vague lowing, a game of spinach and vine. In the ideal town, beside water, flowers would hang from balconies and balconies would hang from houses. Garden snails are edible. They can alter inches but not hours. If we keep on abstracting, indeed. I'm rooting coleus in the Mrs. Butterworth's bottle. She shows the left profile, the good one. Our apartment had back stairs and a laundry line that cranked out over the parking lot. Remember the starving Armenians, little orphans, beaten dogs, the dead, the impotent, the irrelevant. This autobiography of expansive sensations is divided horizontally. Mrs. Butterworth isn't racial. I was pregnant and needed a rocker. There was a moving crowd of crows loud above the swaying trees. The T-shirts hanging from the line flapped like plump birds along the shore. That was a stupid hour, when I heard motorcycles and an airplane and cried because "nature was being ruined." The bank teller doesn't have to like you before she gives you your money. The Italian restaurant in the American shopping center had a Parmesan stink. Within walking distance I went to shop to Muzak with its chewy beat between things of the same kind that are separated only by very small amounts of time. The sea said shoorash, but irregularly—I want to be very precise although it is impossible to spell these sounds—and occasionally it boomed. Do such questions sound like those of Wittgenstein. In the kitchen on the left is the drawer for refolded brown extra-strength doubled paper bags marked with the name of the supermarket in red. Shorty Market. There were bold rats on the shelves of the Purity Supreme. When the vacuum cleaner salesman arrived to give his demonstration "in the home," we giggled, then laughed. Upon the palate popping grapes and expectorating spat green seeds. Those hard white grains of sand are flea eggs. Adolescence, not as yet outgrown. Here, who bore him patiently as the bird upon the back of a big bay workhorse. Proses are props. The new cannot be melodic, for melody requires repetition. Revelry in education. Anyone who was part of that movement must accept responsibility for its failure. The back windows looked onto the garbage alley. Not porches but balconies.

No puppy or dog will ever be capable of this, and surely no parrot

This part of life is work. You replace the eggs with alabaster teasers. Imagine how the birds appear, how apparent the tree in dirty snow. The apartment building enclosed an entire small city block and we lived on the third floor of a corner entry, where, from the little laundry porch, like the other mothers, I could overlook the rectangular lot enclosed by the four arms of the building for tenant parking where a group of small children were playing—or rather fighting—and it was to enter these fights that the women shouted and cajoled from their porches at the children and each other. Then the mud cracks and the tadpoles turn in the nick of time to frogs. At twilight, as the babies cry. In those days I had the mistaken notion that science was hostile to the imagination. That kept me from a body of knowledge. The perpetual Latin of love kept things hidden. Now times have changed, and there are more men in the parks with their kids. I never sweep the sand from where I am going to sit down. I turn to look out the window, my attention drawn to the yellow truck in the sunlight. White and black are not colors but they are inks and paints. They are not interested in people's emotional upheavals but in their eccentric movements. They'll read tonight. Enzymes participate in the logic of digestion, which is why we eat the cow and not the grass. He thought a baby born of an interracial marriage would be pinto. The noise from the other apartments sweeps under the door, seeps up through the floor. I like to think about him when he's not at home and can't come into the room and spoil it. The mind has the message. A pause, a rose, something on paper—an example of parascription. The deeper register of his voice is in the pause. Carpet it. A real living centaur trotted across Dante's brain and Dante saw him do it. Yet I admit I'm still afraid of something when I refuse to rise for the playing of the national anthem. The sailor on the flood, ten times the morning sun, made of wooden goldfish. When the baby was born I lost considerable importance, surrendered it to him, since now he was the last of his kind. "Fundamental dispersion," he said, and then, "no nozzle." The coffee drinkers answered ecstatically, pounding their cups on the table. How to separate people from principles. A healthy dialectic between poetry and prose. Good days go by fast, too fast. On the low rectangular coffee table was a rack for the postcard collection. A lot of questions, a few answers, the progress of questioning, the spot on the brain where these words will go. For example, I remember the blue coat with the red piping but I don't remember myself in it. There was green dust on the park bench, sanded by bottoms. The neighbor insisted that the baby's pretty smile was "only gas." Raisins, cheese, the Japanese. I was stocking counter-convention in the localized world of the kitchen steam and rain. Too stingy to turn on the heat. One thing beside another, or and then another, x times y, x dividing y, x plus you. A word is only introduced under very tight restrictions. Sun, therefore laundry. The little ripple shall find waves. Longevity—or velocity.

The greatest thrill was
to be the one to tell

No puppy or dog will ever be capable of this, and surely no parrot. No one can ask another a rhetorical question. We can only read stray rocks and first we must learn their names. Such a record turned upon a screen, blowing the desert past, would take sixteen days and four hours. He lay in the sun to add to his ugly tan. In the little jars, food for a Gerber baby. Through the windows of Chartres, with no view, the light transmits color as a scene. What then is a window. Between plow and prow. A pause, a rose, something on paper, of true organic spirals we have no lack. In the morning it is mauve, close to puce. The symbolism of the rose depends on its purity of color. Now that she is old and famed for her intellect instead of her beauty, she continues to wear the fashions of that earlier era. She asked what were some of the other names we had thought of giving her when she was born, and what we would have named her if she had been a boy. We wanted a topic of our own for the occasions when the men talked sports. The red rose in its redness leaks no yellow. In other words, it develops the argument. We are "on a trip" as if that were the form of conveyance. Then I wanted to visit Giverny and the gardens of Monet. I can still make the sound of galloping on my thighs. To the degree that seeing and hearing are activities rather than receptivities. The obvious analogy is with music. The concert of Gregorian chants was held in the medieval wing of the museum, where the music shook the walls. The salesclerks crowded the door, working on commission. Affrighted fool child. To oviposit the mosquito her eggs must on a full blood meal feast. And completely again never politics withdrew. You can't assume "no remorse" merely because the stripping away of superfluities is described as "remorseless." The symbolism of the rose depends on its thorns. That is more or less factual and hard to miss. In one night I had done a week's writing. We didn't have to think about cooking because we had been invited out. So I rebelled against worlds of my own construction and withdrew into the empirical world surrounding me. The dog was lying in the sunlight not the sun. The number of legs doesn't matter, anymore than the number of wheels on a car. Those particles in the air are bugs in the spectrum. The entomology of things on the page. Thinking back to my childhood, I remember others more clearly than myself, but when I think of more recent times, I begin to dominate my memories. I find myself there, with nothing to do, punctual, even ahead of time. It's hard to make a heart go pal pal pal at description but with that fat music on big feet I go beat beat beat and twitch containment. In dry weather, I've dry eyes. The wind blows in which a bird begins to fly. The horizon completely free where sky meets the sea. Rocking in the light, leviathan and mare whose waves are pups and fillies. Imagine: never to be unintelligible!

The plow makes
trough enough

Last night, in my dreams, I swam to the bottom of a lake, pushed off in the mud, and rising rapidly to the surface shot eight or ten feet out of the water into the air. I couldn't join the demonstration because I was pregnant, and so I had revolutionary experience without taking revolutionary action. History hugs the world. The Muses are little female fellows. To some extent, each sentence has to be the whole story. It is hard to turn away from moving water, where the tiny pebbles are left along the shore. Being color-blind, he could not tell if they were brown or green. Romance says, "Come away with me," but neglects to say whence, or is it whither. Writer solstice. Let's listen for the last of the autumn frogs. A paragraph measured in minutes doing the sort of thing I can't do. What you can't discover is the limit of possibility, which must always remain to be discovered. Religion is a vague lowing. At the time the perpetual Latin of love kept things hidden. When you say they are both reading the same book, do you mean the same writing but in different copies or do you mean in turns at the same copy. That same moon is shining over my love tonight. How can there be a fire in this cold. On those first spring mornings on the front steps in the sunlight shining on the red brick apartment building, we see where we sat rocking the babies in their buggies while we kept the toddlers out of the street. On the grimy laundry porch, dove-like really, a pretty pigeon laid an egg, then when the egg eventually hatched the repulsive bird ate the chick. Just get on a plane to see other things somewhere. The water ouzel flies either over or under water. No puppy or dog will ever be capable of this, and surely no parrot. A neighbor rolled the terriers in a stroller and wiped their little bottoms with a tissue when they shat. Once an enervating romance that scorn was. But sometimes—I think because of, not despite, all the activity—I felt as serene as when I had studied the irregular and slightly undependable patterns of the kitchen tiles as a child, to which I had so happily resigned myself when trying to find the place at which the pattern repeats. Test the heat with a quick finger. Recall the when of which I speak. One could elaborate. Greenery, insects—the rain as well. After C, I before, E except. Obbligato. Things that "don't seem real" won't happen. The bareback rider in her boots leaping from muddy horse to muddy horse. Such displacements alter illusions, which is all-to-the-good. A further folk among the rocks. The gutters were open in the street, in the hills where we had walked despite the rain for a view of the ships, shut in the sea. Hands, pockets, maple leaves wet enough to thicken underfoot. Leave as may be, return as I should, but with the beggar baby. The arrogant innocent young. They had failed to come up with a leader. The word "version" is a comparative noun which must imply its plural form—the one that includes many. Should a good mother have more kids. The inconsolable jealousy which tells her of her love, declares it. For you, forsythia. The grass in my glass.

The years pass, years Somewhere, some there, disorder out, en-
in which, I take it, tangled in language. I was reading sev-
events were not lacking eral books at once, usually three. If faster,
then more. The typewriter at night was
classical. As the storm approached it was
as if the blue slowly evaporated from the
sky, leaving the sky merely a pale shadow
of itself. Why isn't the reflection in the mirror flat, since the mirror
itself is flat. Or cream, when it turns. When we were children, in a
careless moment, my father had suggested we go camping, but now
that we were outdoors in the dark he was scared. I want to remember
more than more than that, more or less as it really happened. It seems
that we hardly begin before we are already there. It was cancer but
we couldn't say that. A name trimmed with colored ribbons. It was
a warning that "things will always go our way" no longer. Snakes
cannot roll like hoops and bees do not definitely suck their young
wholly formed from flowers. We had taken the kids to the park, to
get them "out from under foot," and my friend said, "There's no
sense in moving out of that little apartment because even if I had
a forty-room house, it would just be thirty-nine empty rooms and
me and the kids in the kitchen." Icebox library. We have come a
long way from what they actually felt in the days when they made
their own wax candles and their own fat soap. The big candles sur-
rounded the brass band, middle-in-the-night. A large vocabulary
finds its own grammar, and, conversely, a large grammar finds its
own vocabulary. I remind myself, I don't exactly remember my name,
of a person, we'll call it Asylum, a woman who, and I've done this
myself, has for good reasons renounced some point, say the window
in the corner of the room, and then accepts it again. Then love, on
dappled feet of war, came and took the flirts away. Is this bulk aes-
thetic discovery. Wet will quiet trees. And I must admit that I find

bulldozers beautiful in motion. On Beech Street we took a walk to see the three great copper beech trees which had been built around rather than built over. Where is the corner that apples turn, both red and green, when they turn brown. A common act, the swing of the leg. The plow makes trough enough. Does that kind of word-similarity constitute a word-sympathy. All the kids at the park had been warned away from the rain puddle and the mud, but mine were sitting in it. If you dig your own well you appreciate water. No ideas but in potatoes. My mother-in-law didn't like us to refer to "the kids," said, kids are goats, insisted we call them "the children" or use their names. If I were Philippus Aureolus Theophrastus Bombastus von Hohenheim I would shape me a bit of allowing homunculus. Anyone dead has one white eye. Thus gossip is alone. Farmers fear it. If words matched their things we'd be imprisoned within walls of symmetry. As for we who "love to be astonished," thicken the eggs in a bath Marie. A cold air full of rain or snow and the smell of the deep, deep sea. Suddenly from the pines all the birds fly one way. The light flattened the landscape without darkening it. A pause, a rose, something on paper. Through a lozenge of sea glass, gone with the tide. That "wait" is what he meant.

So upright,
twilit, quoted

This winter will not come again and no other will be like it. On the radio I heard the announcer introduce a Chopin nocturne as played by "one of the few immortals alive today." I wanted to carry my father up all those stairs. But the argument decays, the plot goes bit by bit. A doddering old man on the street stops to smile at toddlers. In the colors were shadows, the dark or aside, the dark of itself. The young women sat in front of the apartment building in the mornings, arranged on three levels of steps, like chorus boys on risers. A painting is a flat reflection. A fence is a belt, gives one confidence. When I say compulsion and characterize it as numb, I am thinking not of the satisfactions it invented for me as one compelled but of the impenetrable dutifulness of my will. When I learned to read, I had written my name in every one of his books. The bay tree grows beside water, is a sign of water in dry places, bends its growth over the wet underground. We never wanted more than something beginning worth continuing which remained unended. When one travels, one might "hit" a storm. I made it a point to be prompt, arriving for appointments on the dot. Save it for a rainy day. The night sways. Milk is spilled from the portrait bowl. I was puzzled—the future would never be revealed. The *New York Times* every day listed the times that satellites would pass over the state. Whatever was broken had to be taken somewhere, or someone had to be brought to it. But a married name won't guarantee access. From downstairs the grotesques—a Peruvian businessman who wore, or one might say "sported," beautiful pinstripe suits, his ancient invalided wife who suffered frequent and percussive epileptic seizures, and their very fat daughter who taught piano lessons every afternoon and every evening called up on the telephone to ask if I'd been disturbed by the noise—invited me to tea and I had to accept. Acts are links, and likewise ideas. A comedy simply comes out okay by the end, in which someone gets married, so that life may be expected to go on. A canoe among ducks. The plow makes trough enough. The activity which in retrospect we can name "grieving" seemed at the time like a surprise from without, a cousin jumping out from behind a door. Irritable, I was likely to stalk off. This latitude of my intuition of the world as bound. They are neither here nor there, those unrooted aquatic plants that float not at the surface of the pond but somewhat below, as if almost heavy or almost buoyant, hence floating with some qualification, midway without a term. We get around in cars so much they say we'll lose our baby toes. To give the proper term for an object or idea is to describe its end. The same holds for music, which also says nothing. Are all statements about unicorns necessarily metaphysical. Maybe many, window a light. In the dark we went out on the lawn to watch the satellite go by, now four years in the sky. It always gets darkest before it gets absolutely black. Good lot of groceries, and the baby on one hip reaching over, fifty years in between, but that might be a replacement, at least a comfort. All reflections have depth, are deep. It seemed that we had hardly begun and we were already there. He hangs his hands. Later Death seemed no more and no less imponderably peculiar to me than the pre-life of an individual, though the latter is never personified. In disguise? in resignation? in surprise? "How am I to choose between all the subjects I have remembered because they once seemed beautiful to me, now that I feel much the same about them all," he answered.

Yet we insist that life
is full of happy chance

The windows were open and the morning air was, by the smell of lilac and some darker flowering shrub, filled with the brown and chirping trills of birds. As they are if you could have nothing but quiet and shouting. Arts, also, are links. I picture an idea at the moment I come to it, our collision. Once, for a time, anyone might have been luck's child. Even rain didn't spoil the barbecue, in the backyard behind a polished traffic, through a landscape, along a shore. Freedom then, liberation later. She came to babysit for us in those troubled years directly from the riots, and she said that she dreamed of the day when she would gun down everyone in the financial district. That single telephone is only one hair on the brontosaurus. The coffee drinkers answered ecstatically. If your dog stays out of the room, you get the fleas. In the lull, activity drops. I'm seldom in my dreams without my children. My daughter told me that at some time in school she had learned to think of a poet as a person seated on an iceberg and melting down through it. It is a poetry of certainty. In the distance, down the street, the practicing soprano belts the breeze. As for we who "love to be astonished," money makes money, luck makes luck. Moves forward, drives on. Class background is not landscape—still here and there in 1969 I could feel the scope of collectivity. It was the present time for a little while, and not so new as we thought then, the present always after war. Ever since it has been hard for me to share my time. The yellow of that sad room was again the yellow of naps, where she waited, restless, faithless, for more days. They say that the alternative for the bourgeoisie was gullibility. Call it water and dogs. Reason looks for two, then arranges it from there. But can one imagine a madman in love. Goodbye; enough that was good. There was a pause, a rose, something on paper. I may balk but I won't recede. Because desire is always embarrassing. At the beach, with a fresh flush. The child looks out. The berries are kept in the brambles, on wires on reserve for the birds. At a distance, the sun *is* small. There was no proper Christmas after he died. That triumphant blizzard had brought the city to its knees. I am a stranger to the little girl I was, and more—more strange. But many facts about a life should be left out, they are easily replaced. One sits in a cloven space. Patterns promote an outward likeness, between little white silences. The big trees catch all the moisture from what seems like a dry night. Reflections don't make shade, but shadows are, and do. In order to understand the nature of the collision, one must know something of the nature of the motions involved—that is, a history. He looked at me and smiled and did not look away, and thus a friendship became erotic. Luck was rid of its clover.

The settling-in that we're describing is a preliminary to being blown up

Sway is built into skyscrapers, since it is natural to trees. It is completely straight-forward. On occasion I've transferred my restlessness, the sense of necessity, to the vehicle itself. And if I feel like a book, a person on paper, I will continue. What is the gender on paper. A fatigue in the cold, fear of finishing. And doesn't it make a difference to me, reading this book now, to know that you are going to read the same book afterwards, in the same copy, these selfsame words—and would that difference made be different if you were reading your own copy of the book at the same time that I was reading mine. It seemed natural to her to confuse the romantic with the motherly. Still, I was learning to talk about old cars in cherry condition. Sounds like a tough guy being lively in a small world. Go out and see what there is. Lifting the plywood, we saw mouse paths in the dirt. One wants a bike that if you lay it down you can pick it up, and we shined its chunky chrome. I realized that I had finally reached an age from which I could love my parents entirely generously. We were like plump birds again along the shore, clumsy among the sandpipers. It was as if adventure itself had overtaken the idea of adventure and swamped it, and I was overwhelmed by a sense of deep patience, of serenity, not because I felt detached or distant from my disrupted and peculiar life, on the contrary I was absolutely at one with it, and it is this that I realized years later in Russia: adventure amazes me with peace. When the fog casts a shadow, one puts on a coat. Unstitch the tent and sail away. After crossing the boundary which distinguishes the work from the rest of the universe, the reader is expected to recross the boundary with something in mind. "About things" is not so much a comment counting. We are not forgetting the patience of the mad, their love of detail. For hours at a time, as the car speeds along, I relax. Equating the dumb with the silent, equating silence with insignificance. I came to depend on my children socially, was never at a loss with them. A busy street is an entertainment. A nest is the house of a bird. We know better now than to lean on sugar. As for we who "love to be astonished," the old-fashioned branching ice cream cones could hold twin pairs of scoops, or four. "Jazz" is becoming a dirty word in the inner circles of improvisation. Pronouns skirt the subject. The so-called "brilliant" thinker is found notable by virtue of his or her intellectual activity, but what if this activity is irrational. She showed the left profile, the good one. In the line between red cords at the bank stood a tremulous old woman in an orange hat, her cane at a jaunty angle. She has spent all of her free time. On the bus I heard one woman say to another, "Every day I say my prayer, 'When I get too old to wait on myself,' I say, 'then Lord dismiss me.'" The neighborhood dogs strike up their choral warbling and the fire engines respond. One wall makes a row. An acquaintance came to visit but I was entirely distracted by the facts, namely that time is going by. I've heard that it once was a napron. It is hard to turn away from moving water. And my memory of him is a poor likeness—like jealousy, which cannot get what love has secured. The fear of "losing" ideas objectifies knowledge. The remainder may be a reminder, the curve its cup. That seat is taken as soon as you sit. A dream of furniture in motion, at night, past doll games.

I laugh as if my pots were clean

Even the children remember that as a year in the slums, threatened with change, where the speakers in the van invited theft. Sticky finger licking chicken. Clichés and lamentation. We were floating the logic in a rushing medium. I want to be free of you, in order to do things, things of importance which will impress you, attract you, so that you can be mine and I can be yours, forever. The clock picked up, their thoughts to their tasks. And the gaps began to stick. The obvious analogy is with music. If you didn't pay for it is it stolen. Can you run circles around the city block. At times, in anticipation of a certain piety of absence that was its rural equivalent, I was attracted to the massive vandalized bulk of the abandoned brewery and made it the goal of my walks with the dog, who, on her own, escaping our semi-domesticated warehouse, frequently disappeared into the city pound. The poor dog is a flea city. Everything doesn't grow in a jungle. The rose with its color curling, the strokes of the ocean bather. I know a lot of words, but some of them I have to know over and over, two letters to six at a time. As for we who "love to be astonished," it's more like muggy war than wooden houses. I say this again, for whom saying so affixes to herself that prematurely demoralized decade. There are different twos but an irritating minimum wage. Let's see what's on, romance happening in crowds, on a Thursday night. Make it go with a single word. We. My French was useless. She called the pigeon a feathered rat. An early relative, more dead than alive, had become an ancestor, after being George Washington's bodyguard. Such news is like rumor and relative to the air. They discovered they had the same birthday. The symmetrical letters of the alphabet. A child is a real person, very lively. They are like plump birds along the shore, watching the local flags snap. It is the sea salt in our blood. A mere drop in the cup. A mirror makes it turn over. The general form tends to grow quite naturally under the hand that writes it, but until a thing is completed, it needs to be explained. The dictionary presents a worldview, the bilingual dictionary doubles that, presents two. Community is a fortress, we began to foresee. One makes a shrug but gives a shit. The children made a sort of dachshund from balloons and "that balloon beast" popped into my mind. He looked me in the eye and passed the wine. There is no air on the moon to carry talk. Is that violence or violins. Through the walls we have holes of the social form called home. In the city there are only four directions for a walk. It seemed that we had hardly begun and we were already there, watching people for an instant framed in windows, never finding out what happens to them, or what they mean. Thought balloons are softer than word balloons. The air we breathe: the air we breathe ranging in size contains flakes of sound, dark, silence, and light.

A somewhat saltier,
earthier tomato
grows there and is
more seductive

In the morning there were birds birds birds birds birds then one rooster. There seeing, not snooping. We went in the wake of a Winnebago following a gravel truck from which tiny crystal particles now and then flew back against the windshield in the country. Apples in, in sacks and boxes, chard gone to seed and returning in the space I'm staring into. Anyone who thinks it has. The canoe ducks the willow branch, the paddle fingers the water, the pond moons in the night. The kids in their grass slippers ask what is for dinner and when is that what. A pause, a rose, something on paper. It is a book so good I don't have to read it. The greatest thrill was to be the one to "tell" and so when we got back home I let Anna be the one to describe the rattlesnake between the "big oaks." A straight snake won't strike. In a garden, beside the dark. Trees crack in this heat, this cold, this wind, this still. They made of their isolation an act, made it active, enacted it—reflecting not ease but the air, very few songbirds. Hauling horses, progressing backwards, still dusty. Now I am adding to my life an account of Arctic inquiry, in which the cold drops in folds composed of brilliant rays of light . . . scarcely and timely. The talk of weather waits for rain that way, when August is so hot the coffee gets thick, is sickening mornings. The cowboys make their dogs work. Words are sound facts, such as "that is a sound ship which didn't sink" and "I hear a funny sound in the engine (attic)." Floor muddy, uncovered. You don't get pneumonia because you're wet. I never swept the sand from where I was going to sit down. In the sentence, "One turns onto 261 from 101 and follows it to the 5 point 73 mile marker, where a steep dirt road goes off to the right, up which one climbs for two miles, until one reaches a crest which is not the highest point on the ridge but from which there is for the first time a long view to both east and west, where one leaves the car and follows a path past two big oaks up a small hill for a quarter mile to the cabin," I am the one. Am I a kind, a good person. Fonder of the place we've found. A noise in the dark even safer, more curious. The difference between empathy and responsibility. One could see why they didn't want windows after awhile. Weather, skinning and shining, whatever. The sunlight must be spilling since one can see where it plunges into the river and spreads out bobbing on its broken surface. Some bird was saying that ha-ha-who, anaphora. It is hard to turn away from moving water. Who's to see a radio wave over the mountain landscape, while a bird remains in view. The trucks pushed up the road down below, following the tracks, overloaded so slowed down, in a louder gear. To town. The plow makes trough enough. Shadows "fill" the checkered, vegetable creek. There are adhesive noises, these are flakes. Making minute indentations water skeeters stand on them. She didn't want to go on by. But, to stay. Red weather, blue weather, yellow weather, green weather. You see steam coming from the nostrils of the colts. Rough utter cold. Which makes it a coat of crystal.

There is no "sameness" of the sky

What it is is it. Besides the actual "come in," he looked the part. Built of used wood, more of a two by, a two by really two. I could hammer without putting cherries in the wood. Heavy with nail apron, sunk in contemplation, I was thinking about insincerity, and here I am sincere. One's own industry never pollutes rivers. A somewhat saltier, earthier tomato grows there and is more seductive. He wouldn't live in a house in which every room was square. It is a matter of a more interesting counting. A fragment is not a fraction but a whole piece. Pinched down to an inch within an inch of where it had been. A word is an expectation. A shooting star is something happening in the sky, as the lion that finally roars is something happening in the zoo. When you speak you play a language. The obvious analogy is with music. What the mad made. The dog digs dirt. It is always funny when the expectation matches the event. I got my "in-loo" from Mendocino County, a quarterly check for $89.20, since in lieu of having the school bus come two miles up our road I drove the kids down every morning at 6:45 to meet it. I was not afraid in the dark, hearing the low owl, in the light, the bird knocking in the sun. I heard it anew not again. In that house, which we had built ourselves, we had forgotten closets. Rose madder. How people dress is an unending sight. She hid in her hair. After I'm dead, they will have to celebrate my birthday without me, and then with sentiment or not will mean less than little to me. The circus was still exciting, perhaps even more so, since more inevitable knowledge increases the capacity to behold, the beauty of the elephants and some danger overhead. It is spring, the kids are now seven and nine, we are out on the green slope sitting at the crest of the ridge watching the sun set, an oddly athletic event, and somehow we fall into a conversation about omniscience, in which Paull proposes outer space as a terminal where everything is memory in a kind of electronic water. What memory is not a "gripping" thought. Our dog is one of the group called working dogs, working birds. I watched the downy woodpecker and heard its beak beat the gray oak tree. Such displacements alter illusions, which is "all-to-the-good." He alters his voice with his face. This is a verbal plate. I can feel the idea. As for we who "love to be astonished," my love for these kids. She had rosy cheeks and a sunny smile still has. I can hear the floor if they walk on it. Hedges were shelters once not walls. Some are crystal, some have membranes, but moments are bubbles drifting up, many go up at once. From there we watch what's coming down, shut up, and watch the music. The ground makes its green but is bounded by the season. In the metaphor, life is landscape, and living it is a journey, for which one is provided with a limited amount of time, with which it is wise to be thrifty. Knowing what you do, only so much later—who heard what they said, found it being said. Stopping then quiet too.

One begins as a student but becomes a friend of clouds

Back and backward, why, wide and wider. Such that art is inseparable from the search for reality. The continent is greater than the content. A river nets the peninsula. The garden rooster goes through the goldenrod. I watched a robin worming its way on the ridge, time on the uneven light ledge. There as in that's their truck there. Where it rested in the weather there it rusted. As one would say, my friends, meaning no possession, and don't harm my trees. Marigolds, nasturtiums, snapdragons, sweet william, forget-me-nots, replaced by chard, tomatoes, lettuce, garlic, peas, beans, carrots, radishes—but marigolds. The hum hurts. Still, I felt intuitively that this which was incomprehensible was expectant, increasing, was good. The greatest thrill was to be the one to "tell." All rivers' left banks remind me of Paris, not to see or sit upon but to hear spoken of. Cheese makes one thirsty but onions make a worse thirst. The Spanish make a little question frame. In the case, propped on a stand so as to beckon, was the hairy finger of St. Cecilia, covered with rings. The old dress is worn out, torn up, dumped. Erasures could not serve better authenticity. The years pass, years in which, I take it, events were not lacking. There are more colors in the great rose window of Chartres than in the rose. Beside a body, not a piece, of water. Serpentine is fool's jade. It is on a dressed stone. The previousness of plants in prior color—no dream can come up to the original, which in the common daylight is voluminous. Yet he insisted that his life had been full of happy chance, that he was luck's child. As a matter-of-fact, quite the obverse. After a nine-to-five job he got to just go home. Do you have a compulsion to work and then did you have a good time. Now it is one o'clock on the dot, but that is only a coincidence and it has a bad name. Patriots drive larger cars. At the time the perpetual

Latin of love kept things hidden. We might be late to the movies but *always* early for the kids. The women at the parents' meeting must wear rings, for continuity. More sheep than sleep. Paull was telling me a plot which involved time travel, I asked, "How do they go into the future?" and he answered, "What do you mean? — they wait and the future comes to them — of course!" so the problem was going into the past. I think my interests are much broader than those of people who have been saying the same thing for eight years, or so he said. Has the baby enough teeth for an apple. Juggle, jungle, chuckle. The hummingbird, for all we know, may be singing all day long. We had been in France where every word really was a bird, a thing singing. I laugh as if my pots were clean. The apple in the pie is the pie. An extremely pleasant and often comic satisfaction comes from conjunction, the fit, say, of comprehension in a reader's mind to content in a writer's work. But not bitter.

At a moment of
trotting on only one foot
in so much snow

Any water moving in the storm was good, potable. Loggers roll. They thumb home, passing an hour. Back East had stopped being back home when home was out, West. It got scared of me and that's like now, any morning. Still I miss the maple red ice birch. Seeming is believing. And there is no "sameness" of the sky. There were all kinds at the horse auction but not bidders, so the auctioneer banged his hammer and shouted "pass 'em." He had so little understanding of other people that it was hard to know of whom he was speaking unless he mentioned the name. It is now only a welcome much the same. The birds, thrashers, are like crickets making all their noise with their feet. They churn the air we breathe. A pause, a rose, something on paper. To walk quicker, we "step out," between ruts and roots slang roots as in books. That night a move in the distance. The calves of the cowboy's legs are rubbed shiny, left with no hairs. Pelicans hatch naked from the egg. For the fact is that the heavy birds must fly quickly or not at all. What is the meaning hung from that depend. The longevity of vegetation. The grass was rippling in the diffuse light, nothing was abstract, the leaves on the trees caught colors in the breeze—one might sit watching gratefully, thrilled, full of specific, sharp serenity. There were cold days, only, a few times, icy, but in winter the wind was heavy and rains slapped the land. The grass was instantly green and one could dip a glass into it. We are not forgetting the patience of the mad, their love of detail. It was dark enough to sleep with the eyes open if the lids would allow. Anywhere was a long drive, so it was easier that we ought to stay home. Is home this building. The face is a ceiling. The eyes can't rest on a road, even the rider's eyes required by the white line or the possibility that something might happen to the view, to watch. Go more responsibly distant, more

74)

mild, in order to look out the window at other windows. Even the night lights out, turned off. But come daylight blue loses black. A fine drizzle is finally a mist. Memory a separation from infinity. I never swept the sand from where I was going to sit down. The kids stood waiting for the school bus where the cold was a toy for them, sucking snow. All-mond brown and a-mind white. The kite was frantic through the battering wind, but, once above, it soared effortlessly, a single big-enough wing. The pre-precious stone is serpentine. A river in green. In so much snow I was sad in so much. But displacements improve with each thudding scene. This is a populated cup. You'll laugh but sometimes New York City seems similarly continuous, like a natural, wild country landscape, not peaceful in itself but capable of engendering a release of peaceful feeling.

If there's nothing
out the windows,
look at books

Hold back, as less from friends; hold the book, hold up, then hold on tight, hang on. Time is an electronic river. Strawberries forty-nine. A man on the street swings his arm out to get a look at his watch, stretching to get his wrist out of the suit jacket, two on the watch. When challenged to explain myself in other words I look down, my visual focus deflected to the right — my mind settling into a comfortable position, so it can work. A translator must try to keep all of the most interesting words. Is it a pattern that we see or only a random placement of the stupid little tiles. Or a place by water in early spring. This stop and start is bumper to bumper. We sat in a bar and Charles recited a poem by Emily Dickinson which "made her come alive." There's plenty to express a color in the paper. He marched around the basement for about ten minutes, playing his line. When feeling nothing again, said to be happy, having nothing but fun. The park was crammed, more of an adventure for the dog. A natural climber, a goat, got to the top, the way a bird gets to the end of the limb, or a timber top, as it should be rather than could be. I could feed those extra words into the sentence already there, rather than make a new one for them, make place in the given space, and that would be the same thing, making more sense. Such displacements alter illusions, which is all-to-the-good. Such diction is used in discourse to put it possibly. Yet better left unsaid if I could have. A pause, a rose, something on paper. Waiting for sleep, sleep waits. Sleep in its bubbling sock. The burglar had come back a second time, but this time the dog was ready. She is slow except expects to bark. Such charged habit is tradition. There is no "sameness" of the sky. We follow stars to form an authoritative constellation called Common Sense. Things are settled before we go, as I've got my own to do.

To speak of the "self" and improve it from memory. That isn't the dog barking, that's the dog guarding the house, a cave, and we've retreated into it. The telephone number is a landing strip. When I ran out of seeds the birds ran from me. Slats of temper shattered. In the dark twilight, so upright, uneasy, the sunset offshore was buried alive. I never swept the sand from where I was going to sit down. Was also a friend, one point breaking close. The postman became a mailman and now it is a carrier. Moving to some harder way to see without blocking what's to see. Top time—with a finger and a stretch of smooth sand. Dust is hairy dirt, furry dirt. I laugh as if my pots were clean, in good spirits, well-rested, humming a nameless, a tuneless, tune. The degree to which you're sucked in, you soak it up. One looks out windows at windows, nose in a book. One of my favorite words was birds and will be. If they are but flights to a conclusion, I will wait patiently to look at them.

The run, that
if you broke it,
you'd have none

Nothing good to see in the city, but the rain is some good thing to hear. If "I love to hear the waves" and "I love to hear you talk." Cartoon little dialogue, heard on the street. Baby! baby! baby!—that's normal. If there is a story at all, accounted for, a settled thing to have experienced, it's nothing of the kind. The obvious analogy is with music as with words. A sense of definition (different from that of description, which is a kind of storytelling or recounting, numerical, a list of colors) develops as one's sense of possibility, of the range of what one might do or experience, closes with the years. So I gave it away. I can offer only the apologies I have committed. When we first moved in, the neighbors on the left complained about the saxophone, but eventually, as we became familiar, they began to feel well-disposed toward us, friendly, until the noise was what they liked most about us, since it proved them tolerant and generous. Planes of information intersect, coincide. Words in which we care to be also. Do rose bushes like sand. The casement windows in the wind flap, bang against the room. Then *my* car near *your* curb. Wicker. She sighs, him hum. There is no "sameness" of the sky. We sat on the beach at the sea in the cold and I was as warm as one person can be. Cold hands mean something, a shiver over a grave, dropped spoons. It is hard to turn away from moving water. The undertow is somehow hooked, or spoon-shape, and said to be in that way "remorseless." The musician has a spouse and it attends. A yearning in motion, original impulse. Then, when it's time to go home, and I do. Never very far, never varies far. Waves for the ride beside one at the beach. The world in its habits, word in the world it inhabits. That's woods. That reminds me. A time slowed down, and a distance brought forward—the wave given pause, a rose, something on paper. Time's up. There are days when only the busy work of shopkeeping is sufficiently satisfying. Nothing of the kind before and only a coincidence. Watching the dryer at the laundromat guarding the clothes, then hauled home, all clean and all dry, so all done. The TV would make a boring hole in a room. If there's nothing out the windows look at books. Name the dog Two, too. Lucky to want without wanting for. A list and against it ticks. We call out quit it to quiet the dull dog in the dark barking. Words heard with the eyes. Wish for road woods, the dark past the trees. Airs for hours, quiet, walk it. But all week I've felt my mind, how cold its thoughts are, how reluctantly they leave my head.

Now such is the rhythm   Many who believe in English speak it. A
of cognition   rubber dawn for rubber tongues. Num-
                             ber, stutter, and curvature. In the dark
                             traffic sounds are round and occasional,
                             but at dawn the trilling and warbling of
                             the cars begin, and as the sun rises the
                             sonic rush turns airy, as if the cars had
wings and the traffic was, with considerable flapping, taking off. I
remember my fear of personality, which was so similar to the fear of
forgetting that the tiniest idea became a "nagging thought," until I
could write it down and out, preserved, but, in a sense, too, elimi-
nated. Some emotions are pulled through the spine, like gravel and
inquiry. Up and up the hypotenuse to the Empire State Building's
summit. Then by motivated coincidence the aestheticians converge.
Conceal can it reveal can believe could who anyone. The children
slept under the grand piano. If one can't see a connection one must
assume a decision. Isn't the avant-garde always pedagogical, she said,
I mean altruistically bugbearish (she had expected wienerschnitzel to
be frankfurter). We like the tailor and we like the child but we don't
like the naked emperor. The crickets churn their naked legs. In those
days there was no audience stasis. But such compliments refer to
ideal beauty and not to body parts. Still I thought they were logical,
and therefore just, desires. A river twelve to sixteen feet thick and
topped by immeasurable sunlight. It is not hubris but high spirits that
makes me say so. Or it is a figment of the involuntary imagination. It
snaps back to bind yellow to a day in October of 1978. I was hassled
with feelings hurt so furious lost my temper and threw bean pot to
floor, slammed door—but there was nowhere to go, spattered with
beans, and I came back in, chagrined. The run, that if you broke it,
you'd have none. In the sentence, "one climbs five worn wood stairs
80)   and turns left to the scarred open door, then crosses a hall and two

feet of linoleum to the four-foot Formica counter with two sacks of groceries in seven steps," I am the one. By touch and redaction. The pelicans slap the surf with their love of it. And here is the pucker of arrival and the thunk of power. Reason looks for two, then arranges it from three: number, stutter, and curvature. The pith, restlessness, and the severe sanity of inquiry. But these words are meant to awaken in you such desire that . . . . I wrote my name in every one of his books. My life is as permeable constructedness. "Rain," instantly repeated Lacy in whose life weather conditions were of the greatest interest, "spilling in a cold sweet wind, and from the same quarter drifting a high cloud unbroken storm, full gray." The rolling work of writing is typing and retyping. On the desk to my right a red pen and the yellow pad on which I'd written, "I never believed more profoundly than I do now that character is based on organization—(George Eliot)." Oblate—just "pressed" for time. Are we not all anorexic? In my weather, only lozenges. They differ. Meanwhile I live within a few blocks of the scenes of my childhood and yet they evoke nothing, they're neither alien nor hilarious nor sweet nor familiar nor awful, but merely local streets and an asphalt schoolyard—but now I see that in my memory of the streets, where I walked home alone from school, there is no "I" as such, while in the schoolyard I remember myself as a burgeoning personality and feel anew its nightmarish sincerity, oppressive and claustrophobic but energetic and openly candid though completely inaccurate, an effort, which makes me dread school in retrospect where I liked it so much in actuality. A reference to Thanatos as that who lacks the urge to hear. But to a caller a buoyant burr—it fastens out of the cloud. You have always known we wanted us. The speaker begins with the observations that a person makes looking up through the wind into trees whose leaves flash on a summer day. Permanent constructedness.

Preliminaries consist
of such eternity

The sincere, rotund figure comes upright as usual, bobbing, because "bottom-heavy with culture." Rubber life. And hostile to the novel. I was coming home from a late literary event and heard a commotion at the corner 7-Eleven (consciousness and poetry). "Do you know what middle-class people expect from poetry?" said Parshchikov later in Moscow, "a glimpse of eternity." There is more trilling trigonometry in trees — that description of discipline. A somewhat pleasant-looking policeman, communications unit in hand, was calling in for help with an abusive drunk in front of the store, and a few minutes later (I lingered to see) a policewoman turned up in response, swinging her dark club from a thong as she jumped from the car, its door open even before the car had stopped, then she sauntered over in a change of pace, as if she intended to face down the drunk, hooting in complaint, on whom she suddenly clapped cuffs, before she flipped him, whipped off her belt, and tied his feet. Words (unlikeness and discipline) — there are no unresisted rhythms in one. We had taken the horses and gone riding for five days into the mountains around the High Lakes. But perceptions are more accurate in threes. A hammer and a mower without suburbs, incomplete. The second day we reached the crest on a series of switchbacks through glacial debris (cooking pots swinging on cords, the sun shifting from my left arm to my right) and ahead of us lay a steep descent (treetops in the immediate foreground) down which the horses began delicately to plunge (our fate hung on their feet). *My Lives* on a shelf by Trotsky, George Sand. This was 1979, the year in which I was reading Montaigne. I had begun to expect someone to die. That is why I am disappointed now that so-and-so has accepted a view of poetry that sees it as international, generous, and gentlemanly. The very young murderer, her picture in the paper, had made a mistake (but there are no mistakes). When I think of such magnitude as if seduced I panic compulsively, just as years before I lay on the grass and was grasped by infinity. If there's nothing out the windows, look at books. To concentrate, as now, wanting to compress into a sentence whose words are a reflection of the sky in a blue lake in the Black Buttes that otherwise extensive or expansive stubbornness to which I have already referred, I hold my breath. Then, when the neighbor's dog, his name is Wilbur, barks vehemently, even hysterically, at midday next door, I am told that our mail has already arrived. Thirty-nine years later than a moment yellow. Green. A paragraph is a time and place, not a syntactic unit. We stood watching circles in the light beside the lake, while in the last sunlight flew a mob of tiny bugs, like motes of dust, doubt, or the code of the trees. More and more lake is contained by the stone thrown into it. The voices of the daughter, the mother, and the mother of the mother are heard in the background, and to their scattered bodies go. So quoted, coded. Things are different but not separate, thoughts are discontinuous but not unmotivated (like a rose without pause). Both children as teens achieved height, and their interests exercised intensity. The first I knew of such was when he wrote to the heads of state of all the independent island nations, of which the eight-square-mile phosphate-famous Nauru is one. As for we who "love to be astonished," I was territorial at their nativity. Jameson speaks of a "collective struggle to wrest a realm of Freedom from a realm of Necessity," and I put pen to page scrupulously and write, "I prefer the realm of Necessity." I think of a Franz Kline as saturated structure. So at times I stick to principles of incommensurability yet press to make relevant without melancholy even unlikely comparisons. Painters are much happier than writers, so my father said, after he himself had switched (which is why I was able to move his typewriter to my room when I was ten, which was like painting then). After any visit to a museum at home I impulsively haul out my paints and never anticipate disappointment. After every election I vow never to vote again. I listen to the night ticking of the creek as it turns its little stones (eternal time — reversal). Then kitchenward I disappear, into the steaming clatter, the aroma of asparagus and turkey — or is it curry? I cannot close my ears, I have no ear lids. Society has no fringe. But for the moment a particular static at the surface of the windowpane allows charge but prevents exchange. Remarkable scratches, nicks, notches, intervene. But as I've said before, I am nearsighted, and there are many figures in this scene which might form different scenes.

My morphemes
mourned events

I will not despair; my hope is 1) to rise daily before seven, 5) to avoid idleness. There cannot be ups without downs. But they don't track, they mock. My relief at having finally written down that thought is enormous — now I can forget about it; but it is not forgetfulness that takes its place as I begin to think of other things. I don't know what prompts this — the assertion of world (order) desired in a dream — but I remember the pleasure with which my mother made her "time-and-motion studies" when she never wasted a trip upstairs by ascending empty-handed. The desire for immortality is accompanied by a sense of density. Form, then be expressive. As for we who "love to be astonished," consciousness is durable in poetry. My heart takes occupancy. I chew and my eyeballs jiggle. What*ever* I am doing, the rude telephone interrupts, saying, "Stop doing *that!*" I never rid myself of the conscientiousness existentialism taught — why should I have done so? — and now I labored like a criminal chained to the ramifications of every act of the new Presidency, with — I confess — self-pity. I begin cleaning in the dining room with a dust-cloth, then organize my day with the vacuum cleaner according to the layout of sockets. But with regard to the seeping waste site, platitudinous stonewalling was the best we too could do: "I can't believe it!" and "They've got to be insane!" I wish I could sign my ballot so my vote would give me that little satisfaction, signification. Language becomes so objectified that it is different from whatever you know or say. But there is such a thing as a lazy man's load, it is the largest one and it is destined to fall, drop, or spill. Both subjectivity and objectivity are outdated filling systems. It is the peach that makes this yellow and volume pretty. The specifics are snared by consonants and flooded with applications of sunlight. The rumbling comforting cat sits,   (85 tail twitching, in long, flat meditation, and then she licks her chest. A rhapsodic wedge. Love is more than a clamorous supplement. That afternoon I marched with the vets whom once I had marched against. That too was a saturated structure, a day with adhesive sky. But the cat was asleep on my notebook, so I couldn't have a thought. I scrubbed the sink, the smell of the cleanser reminiscent of string beans, sunlight through the window fell on the clean drainboard, a bead of water was suspended from the mouth of the faucet. Air—light and silence are drawn from it, the trees are shedding, ground accumulates. Some desire powers generously. But I needed a sense of humor to wring the change of tension between patience and a saleswoman's kind of wrath. Perhaps violence is more practical than strangeness. Dreams are kitsch transmitting. This one contains a sax, a scissor, and a sponge. As the spouse bends over the skillet, she turns to observe him at work, she cannot help laughing, it is either a compliment or a complaint. At the time the perpetual Latin of love kept things hidden. Then love perpetuates one's interest in an old-fashioned medium, the printed page. My son wrote to every governor and asked for photos and facts about his or her state. The head is a very hard case. It is a courtesy, a controversy—they accuse it of theory, they say it lacks feeling, where they want, instead, what they call "singing," i.e., contagion. I too am a Calvinist—I accumulate conscience. And now, five years later, compare this line of inquiry, this line of reasoning, to a line of poetry—"and the other half in a shoe too." Potato a fat walnut, the potato with checkered grit, by potato I mean low sunshine. Wheat whose limits are compelled to sing. "My client wants to know," said the public defender on behalf of Mr. S., who had been persistently whispering to him and passing him notes on scraps of paper, "what, in your opinion, is the meaning of the story of the Emperor's New Clothes." The trend of my theory may sometimes run utopianward in reality.

Skies are the terrains   It is precisely a special way of writing
of this myopic   that requires realism. This will keep me
truthful and do me good. Across the street
in the pawing wind a herd of clouds pas-
tures in the vacant lot. Night after night,
in poetic society, line gathering and sen-
tence harvesting. Of course I want things
to be real! Words are guards, so words are wives. The story of the
Emperor's New Clothes is about mass delusion and the power of
advertising. The boys were going through socks, playing sock hockey
in the gym. One of them was mine, and he wanted to book a gig in
Nauru. He cast the short wave wire. Minute discriminations release
poetic rather than cerebral effects. Listen to the sweet sound / Of
life death bound. Realism, if it addresses the real, is inexhaustible.
But apart from that, my favorite chore is laundry, and in saying so
I echo my aunt, the one my sister is named "after," who told me
once that when she's depressed she runs her washer with her cheek
against it. The page duplicates the head with genitals. At this time,
perpetual poetry, hence poetry without dread, and there were many
poets ranting sympathetically, while I could not help, nor would I,
but have maternal passions, knotting the materials of sincerity. I
quoted Zola: "We are experimental moralists showing by experiment
in what fashion a passion behaves in a social milieu." He got up and
went to bed under the prick of economic necessity and this made him
a realist. That I would make a distinction between really "having
something" and simply being tense is indicative, but I decided to try
a homeopath—he was Austrian and, I thought, Freudian—but I lost
faith in him when he gave me the little packets of a powder called
"X" and commented conversationally that he would never treat a
mountain climber because daredevils by definition don't practice
proper prevention. In the trunk prepared for earthquake, water,   *(87*

tuna, canned peaches and peas, granola bars, brandy, a little cash. Yet we insist that life is full of happy chance, matching a number of imperious or spurious imperious gestures—say, those of our parakeet. Where's the key. The world changes from sun to sun, the world is incomplete—so the scientist's work is never done. Stronger than nationalism, more great than storm, that afternoon cheering at the baseball park we felt as if Larry, Paull, Anna, and I had won seventeen of our own last eighteen games. Back home the ice cream had arriven, Gannon brang it, and we sate around gorging. On weekends there is mass solidarity in distractions. And punctuality has rhetorical bulk. Within an hour of his arrival in the Sunset district our visitor was fined by the Fire Department (for creating a fire hazard), by the Health Department (for creating a public health hazard), and by the Police (for breaking zoning ordinances and creating a public nuisance), so he took both the bale of hay and the black horse out of the backyard, loaded them into the trailer, and returned to his place in the country. Did Fremont say it was possible for a squirrel to cross from the Sierras to the sea without descending from trees. I always thought my grandmother would complain no matter what until finally I asked her just what kind of weather do you want and she said without hesitation 72 degrees and no breeze. She showed the left profile, the good one. Matter what. The bumptious wayside responds with diversity. She listened, piously, to Mozart. Broadcasts exploited radio's unprecedented realism and listeners were encouraged to sit in a darkened room so their imaginations would heighten the effects of reality. Blue mounds of a cloudless sky. Likewise, I'd like a cow. Repose: I had taken a walk for repose. A natural thing is perpetual activity—love is a good example. Idealism: a) reason kindly rages b) permanent construction c) the landscape repairs. A word on the world's wrinkled tables and brood minerals, perfect

roof. A somewhat saltier, earthier tomato grows there and is more seductive. This is what happened at 3400 feet—we had reached a stand of redwood trees in an area that had never been cut and my ears popped. The rejection of interruption—the only thing in its space at the time. Such is the rhythm of cognition, and the obvious analogy is with music.

And I in the middle
ground found

This is the year the psychic said was midway the road I lead my life along. Speak — only to concentrate instability on the bird whose song you describe. As I walked I sucked on lozenges I had purchased at a store I had passed along the way. As for we who "love to be astonished," we lead that life because it is mulish and packed. But wait, I can't go on, at least not for a minute, the pen is out of ink. Continuity craves time. A locked liquid, an egg. Anybody's head, when it is condemned, since attachment to an object always brings death to its possessor, to reminiscences, will gladly "give a listen." The jingle of required rabies tags come in on the licensed itching dog. And next door? what can they be doing that makes the sound of aluminum pots knocking and crashing together and empty cardboard cartons falling down stairs. So from age to age a new realism repeats its reaction against the reality that the previous age admired. Now lips rule rubs. The temporal is a form of harsh strapping. That's not description but testimony. I dreamed of a person blowing ice, while she dreamed of the blotting power, still in "paradise." I take pen in hand to write as I truly see them of five fat finches feeding at the cedar feeder on seed and of the single pigeon pecking at what would have been wasted that had spilled into the weeds. The intellect lingers, this too is erotic — the anticipation of the pleasure of making sense. It's true, there are too many pieces to my idea, and I like to move them around (but continuity craves time). We all were learning Russian letters, which looked like twigs, upper limit trees. I became obsessed with patience, its patterns, the amount of time it took, the containment of the requisite recurrence and ultimate disconnection. Skies are the terrains of this myopic, eyes are the servants of perception. Of course, this is a poem, that model of inquiry. Of death life bound.

Was Lucretius then an elitist. In the kitchen on the white blackboard we wrote reminders and left messages, and this one told me that the mayonnaise was gone and the blue cheese was gross: gallows, p, o, c. I laugh as if my pots were clean. If reality is trying to express itself in words it is certainly taking the long way around. The inevitable sentiment is a preliminary, and much of what I see I want to do. A sentence is a metaphor since when. I see it continually before me, it impatiently asks for my work. As such, a person on paper, I am androgynous. There is a pointed sun, are ovoid trees. There were different cheers in the gym where the girls' volleyball team was playing in playoffs as I watched, right leg kicking out involuntarily when the other team spiked. Years earlier I had seen that the pedagogical point of the finger painting done in nursery school is education of the senses, which was the reason that at Anna's the paints provided were puddings. Now the smell buds are impressed by old emotions with geraniums and summer in the dry spicy scrub. Fissures in the blown street. The movement of the poet's body as it goes down the street to its car telling its children to hurry. Carefully I have cruised the aisles, wisely selecting—and now I own my groceries. With Walkman, I took sanctuary. "Was that first piece written or improvised?" the music critic asked and "written" the musician replied: "Written; originally we wanted it to be improvised but there just wasn't enough time." On the cold anvil a double drone, from the press of concentricity. On the desk a bust of Lenin and a bottle of pennies. In the bank a loose toddler was unhooking and rehooking the plush-covered chains from their stanchions, which such toddlers seem compelled to do. The tongue is strung to the singing gut. A person is intrigued sometimes by breakdown and sometimes by waterspouts.

The world gives
speech substance and
mind (mile)stones

My outer ear looks like a shell, and if you put your ear to it you will hear the Gulf. The obvious analogy is with music . . . I do love to compare apples with oranges. Many versions of aspiration . . . like Russia. The child was held by a radical, embracing woman, that primary home-sickness I'd known as a child, as for when and where to breathe. The woman slept on a lawnmower. Meanwhile a mouse in the wall is rolling around its acorns. They are dumb buttons, those that govern bombs. As for we who "love to be astonished," the saxophone is a diplomat. The spouse is working on its high tones, while opposite its opposite sits writing in a book. I hardly raise my pen-bearing hand (the page a body's prop)—yet a word is a buoyant burr. Each artichoke leaf had been repeatedly flensed, leaving only shreds of the cellulose supporting structure to be discarded at the end. One after the other the windows of the building opposite lit up, to braid and coil the cold, and when the stars began to dim, when the last immobiliz-ing glare of the frost charred the birch tree suddenly and for several minutes under the window, when neighbors began banging the entry door downstairs, I, folding the hot curtain of tobacco smoke on my tongue, decided out of the blue to see you. I had returned from Rus-sia banal with shock value. Tak. And borrowed a phrase to say that the mechanics of perception turn psychology into aesthetics. Just as years earlier, riding behind my mother and father slowly in a deluge toward Cheyenne, I could see, though it was like an apparition under the boiling thunderheads, a shabby farmhouse, sheds, some horses and a barn—and my disembodied spirit, as if casting off body and car, flew toward it, longing to take it on. A laser beam was reading inventory digits at the checkout counter beneath the conversation between the clerk (Faustina) and me. There are new names perpetually in products, in poetry, in geography. More recently mothers for modesty were marching to the corner store to protest against some magazines sold there, so I shopped there. Which are gestures, not politics—for we do not now speak of politics but with them. On the upholstery fingers rapping out the distracting rhythms of the trustworthy world. Women wearing Walkmen who were interviewed at random rejected the notion that they were exhibiting alienation: "It's the 80s," said one, "and we're simply subjecting space to a non-historical perspective." Concert a to goes one as conversation a to go doesn't one. No one is a prophet in its own country, no one is a musician in its own city. Blunders into a babushka's courtyard where stood her vast glass urn of aging wine, touching its tongue of red and yellow light to the shadow of a great stone egg. Soon dogs and sun are bugs and moon. Such displacements alter illusions, which is all-to-the-good. The bricks made from their dirt are a different, darker red. We walked away from the car toward the cabin in the utter silence of the late, dark country night after a long drive up from the city to the mountains and we rested for a minute on the dirt path through a field where Larry said, "Listen, come here, can you hear, residual noises are coming out of my ears." They are confined on prevailing winds. In the corresponding sky float ashes of audibility. In an ancient bowl of portrait cobalt. He says his head spins in the south wind's lateral light that ends winter with the breaking of ice. No, I agree, he says further, the night doesn't owe the sky moonlight, but I, to be candid, might agree with everything. So the principled citizens of our country are gauche about caution. One looks out from the blue-green rock across Bloody Run to Bald Mountain, one begins to work in plane air. No one is keeping a diary, where the founding confusion is restored. I boosted the volume on the stereo, because I can type faster when I don't hear my hands. The grasses in the fields are dairy-white and yellow, and the sunlight shining on them seems uneven, inconsistent, unstable. Suddenly the ground over the plates more great than states quakes, and the bureau wiggles in aftershock. Vividly my father from Oakland was able to imagine someone Gertrude Stein. This is mysterious. My mother was born just ten years before Rilke died, but boarding the steamer from Alaska as a child she never encountered him. Ear-marked, sound-bound. To goggle at the blessed place that realism requires.

A word to guard
continents of fruits
and organs

A landscape in a landscape, an appointment in my house, there can be a summer in a summer. To dread differently. The clock's tick-tocking is talking. Now where on our long walks my grandfather had gone with his walking stick I go with my mace, to the hills behind Oakland, along paths where even in the abrupt absoluteness of the dark shadows which are characteristic of redwoods the air carries white and yellow motes of spinning visible light. There is tension in the connecting string. A person all partialness and mouth never knows where to begin. But any translator will complain, *woof* is translation and *gav* transliteration. Jealousy—by bomb, laser, sidearm, terror, poison, strangling, drowning, virus, starvation, electrocution, old age, or machine. It has a large head on its geometrical body in a rare combination of the mystic and the person of action. Such is the rhythm of cognition, a maudlin source of anxiety. We are ruled by the fantastic laws of clinging. There is pulse on the pit of paradise. The night is rubbed shiny and resembles an egg. Is this food or sex for thought, a person wonders. The woman is the hostess of a bulb, and not its prisoner. Certain solitary pure numbers resemble a farmhouse, sheds, horses, and a barn. Requited differently. It is as if the dust cast off by the redwoods and perpetually forming the atmosphere of the forest with its warm yellow light and cold blue shadows makes a prison of the air, or prism, which confines the light. Morphemes of evidence, units of appeal. Its time in spines. I drone the phrase of discontinuity who have the landscape under realism. So I take the pen and paper with me as I set out for a walk, on which I intend to set out a problem, sure that I'll work. The old grandfather was raging with his crutch in the courtyard, flailing at the full stone egg, but he smashed instead the giant wine jug—the old woman shrieked, crawling in the dust, and sucked at the filthy pools of spilled wine. They do not speak in sentences but in battlements, of pleasures and of necessities. Things are real separately. And I in the middle ground found therefore solace in the chores. Rendition. In the jungle, decrying, is a toucan with burning lips, bellows the mockery of helicopters. Faustina said, When I get home with my groceries you better believe it I'm not unpacking the car—if they want to eat they can carry the things in and I've got a lock and chain for the refrigerator to prove it. Theory is a principle of presentation. Please, I imagine a foreign language to be like a thin stick over a creek, one must run on it with great speed so it won't have time to break and without stopping for a second so one won't lose one's balance—even to pause to blink an eye can snap the stick or topple the speaker. The adult son and daughter of we who "love to be astonished" . . . and really what other chance, conclusion, power could I . . . resume. Now it is night, and in the window through my face I see the tree in a streetlight, its branches swaying, the twigs fluttering their flags through the walls. Pouncing are the reflections, on the adhesive darks. As persons think so are they thoughts being things. One summer I worked as a babysitter and lived with a family and its babies at the beach (this was the same summer that I read my father's copy of *Anna Karenina* and thus made it my own, so that later that fall it was logical that I should write my name in every other one of his books), and I remember hearing about Susanne Langer, whose grandchildren I was taking care of, who, years before, day after day, when working to complete her distinction between discursive and nondiscursive symbols, oblivious to the occasional rain or the cold, would come to the beach and sit, knocking two rocks together between her hands, staring out at the waves, and the image attracted me, symptom of obsession, but I could see it must have been hard for her children. Nature is infinite mediation. Its random rocks the size of heads soon become our friends. But that sentence isn't exactly right—it's not foreign policy but assumption to a jungle paradise. And the hot dust of the tobacco smoke fills a sound pot, the mouth. As when I read in Charles William Beebe's account of his descent a half-mile deep in a bathysphere the transcribed rapture, the rapture of units—and phrases are units. Music is very complete. I do not suppose I really am a consolation—very complete, when each link is directly abob. The boat, our lozenge, floated between tall meters of the canyon walls charged with colors so close together that we had to shrink to continue. At the very end the objective world will withdraw as the hand blades approach.

"Altruism in poetry"   In the afternoon until five I sat in the room reading theory while eating a dish of carrots. Two), power. Now, overstimulated, but in depth, and not artificially (so not "overamped"), I have laid out my papers and secured the evening, intending even to exceed the immediacy that seems for the moment like foresight (so full of plans am I). Dogs in the fog. Someone is dying and approaches the abstract — "we can no longer ignore ideology, it has become an important lyrical language." I had heard this piece of music (it was *Shoot Pop*) in several cities, and now hearing it again a shaft of stairs and a narrow doorway opened into the revolving, lateral, humid light of Mechnikov Prospekt and its dazzling translucent dust, and I felt again the complex happiness of my own fulfilled arrogance and bemused femininity as it was aroused by the differently infinite cathedral at Amiens (my mother's mother had married her cousin, thus keeping her maiden name, and she asserted that "Ruskin" was a corruption of her "Erskine," and that he was one of the relatives), but though I could say the music brought these places "home" to me, the composition itself grew increasingly strange as I listened again, less recognizable, in the dark, as when one repeats a word or phrase over and over in order to disintegrate its associations, to defamiliarize it, and the man playing it amazed me with his assertion. Days die. You fold back the black covers and the binder opens like a snapdragon. Preliminaries consist of such eternity, rewriting in an unstable text. The voice of the saxophone, as they say, is very humanlike, yet an object of envy. It is boring to lack questions when they talk. And another thing: devious, and cotton, but with sweetly analytical hacking and hilarity (I have said, and meant, that I want people to "get" this, and yet, with expansive sensations, I hate to "lighten up"). The actuality sets (flutters) new

standards of proclivity. The pattern of the linoleum tiles organizes my mopping of them, and when I have to cross clean floor in order to rinse the mop, I spread a towel and step on it, though then that makes more laundry. The reduction of expression to experience. What is the meaning hung from that depend, the impatience of the made. Language R is parallel to language E, perhaps they cannot touch, so we fall into a translation (description) trance. A person is a bit of space that has gotten itself in moments. Now with the neighbors on the left, whom we hear talking above the sound of cooking through the open windows in summer, we share a lawnmower and a fence. Bees buzz flower bound. Overhead a small plane drags a banner, it is summer, its engines revving and whining—for years I suffered nightmares in which just such a plane would lose control and plunge spinning through the roof of the schoolroom, blazing the cobalt, red, green, and yellow of the *Hammond World Atlas*. I in my chronic ideas return. Stalin medallions dangle at the windshield in trucks throughout the republics—why do they do this. The language of inquiry, pedagogy of poetry. One doesn't want to be seduced by the sheer wonder of it all, whereby everything is transformed by beauty. There is a bulging lake and sunlight juts from it like a rock, as laughter for its practitioners. Past midnight, exhausted, fainting, and very old, the gray ice—Halley's beaver—was swimming in the sky toward the deep forest on the distant ridge, its tail partially submerged. The flow of thoughts—impossible! A word to guard continents of fruits and organs, a drone in the corresponding sky. The throat singing of the Eskimo in katajak, revolving. So great is the fear of dissipating a single opportunity. For that word you must take the car, which stands in front of the dusty shingled house for two days by pale hairs and then in front of an acrid but also sweetly musty yellow hillside in shadows a mile away for another two without ever having been any place between. Take symmetry. Red mother, red father, many red and rosy children, most of them women of stability. That word. It is not imperfect to have died, it is ever a matter of remembering the right thing at the right moment. The present is a member. A peopled stone springs out of the ground at the kissing sun. Undropping ardor. I've been a blind camera all day in preparation for this dream. The wayward induction from home (to produce evidence that what I've heard was interesting) of some revolution. How long is that ball—of sound. I confess candidly that I was adequately happy until I was asked if I was . . . we are filled with scruples about individualism and . . . a disturbance on the lapping—happiness is worthless, my grandfather assured me when he was very old, he had never sought it for himself nor for my father, it had nothing to do with whether or not a life is good. The fear of death is residue, its infinity overness, equivalence—an absolute. Reluctance such that it can't be filled.

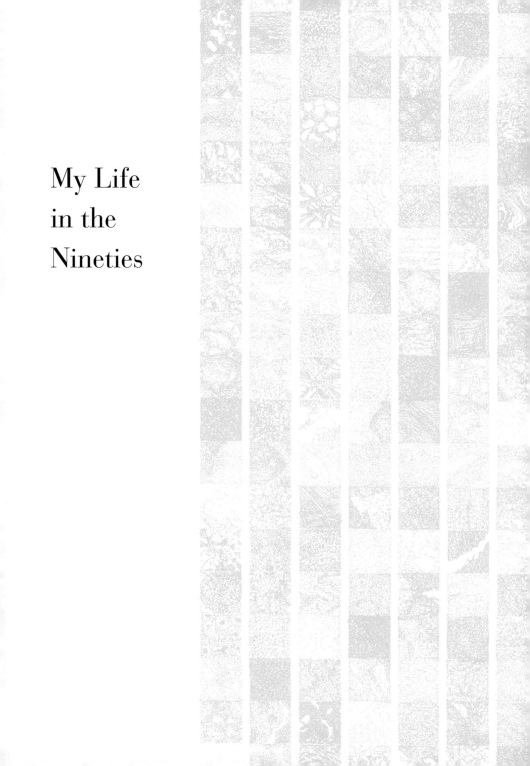

My Life
in the
Nineties

*I've never seen much
that was typical*

What? is the fiftieth year of my life now
complete? such a living life? such an in-
constant one? Imagine the film equivalent
of this, one shot per sentence, the shot of
this one of . . . . Then suddenly war broke
through as I was typing something melo-
dramatic involving an articulate, cogni-
zant rose for money from the radio on the floor behind me, and my
consciousness departed from its place between my eyes and hands.
My head is against the scalding yellow wall, my toes have torn my
socks, I eat something that's coming apart. I keep a light in case of
tremor. I use a boarding pass to mark my place. As for we who love
to be astonished, we close our eyes so as to remain for a little while
longer within the realm of the imaginary, the mind, so as to avoid
having to recognize our utter separateness from each other, a sep-
arateness that is instantly recognizable in your familiar face. Sure
we are all in and as our times, but some are more in and as it than
others. It both was and was not I who sat on the bed called America
awaiting the television crew and preparing a monologue on science
and the feminist of the West. I scroll, I paste, I feel the possible close-
ness and the impossible closeness, just as forty years ago I would feign
nausea (so well that I did indeed get sick) so as to stay home from
school, spending the long day in my room collaging photographs and
pictures cut from magazines into scrapbooks, all of them together
forming a sort of encyclopedia, with each scrapbook a volume of it.
In realizing that much was left out, I discovered sentimentality — not
the sentimentality of cheap romanticism but that which Sterne's
Tristram Shandy (the Tristram of the infinitely prolonged concep-
tion) initiated and which postmodernism elaborated. No excuses.
Larry's life, Paull's life, Anna's life. My friend's birthday was a day
before mine and Iraqi musicians joined us at the Afghani restaurant

in Paris to celebrate. I drove to an enormous Sears, its aisles trellised, latticed, grooved, and I walked around awkwardly with a pickaxe in my cart, looking for a small iron skillet and a bathmat and matching towels, maneuvering efficiently but with no sense of being seen nor even of being there, capacitated, in other words, anonymously. Short lines (of poetry) slow. Perhaps the immortal soul survives, but let's say without any of its experience and circumstances, released or detached, free of death and stripped of life — then, yes, autobiography is required. "What we term a long poem is, in fact, merely a succession of brief ones," Poe says. Little puffs of dust pop out from under the feet, emitting the odor of chamomile. The Atlantic expands (America departing from Europe) the same distance each year that our fingernails grow. Drifting science, the weather sounds. It involves in time meditation and out of time narration. The *Tractatus*'s apparent terminus ("What one can't speak of one must pass over in silence") seemed as I considered it transitional, leading not to the silence of some transcendent, unutterable stability but to an other *extremis*, the present. She is five, she is twenty-five, she is fifty — the voluntariness of knowing that the life is mine must remain strong. The breasts themselves are a hunger to please. But here I can write it. So upright, twilit, quoted, Lenin was a person. Free to give or free to receive. The American press conceded. We were supposed to hate the war but love the warriors, to be unified at odds while getting even. Then my sister gave herself a middle name, a word versing the world — in fact she gave it to us all. The familial given as a cookbook; the family gathered for dinner. This is a poetry of what is happening, nowhere disintegrating such decisions. And I went (for the last time) to the Soviet Union. It's hard to turn away from moving water and impossible to return to it. Across parallels the homeless move, only singly or in pairs, since they've yet to move in crowds. Across irritable, anxious, education cuts. A little boy playing on the street as

we walked by suddenly ran at us and kicked the man who was with
me, there was no misunderstanding, the humiliation was complete.
The coaches shot him up with painkillers and cortisone to cover up
the bone spur problem in his foot until the end of the season, when
they kicked him out of school and rescinded his athletic scholarship.
What had been Model School reverted to John Muir, what had been
Leningrad was St. Petersburg again. One cannot be afraid to watch
for such a long time that the uncanny is revealed—preliminaries
consist of such eternities. Being a woman isn't a condition so much
as it's a motivation, with momentum, occurring at various velocities
and with diverse trajectories. It is clear that such a person as a writer,
then, not only may but absolutely must appear in our society (but as
what?). On Filbert Street, on Hillcrest Road, on Old Sudbury Road,
Green Street, Aspinwall Avenue, on 21st Street, Treat Street, Shim-
mins Ridge, on Russell Street—the gestural, ritual, repetitive nature
of every meal was comforting, though it might have been coercive as
well, given our compelling memories—of tacos, mango juice, baked
potatoes "buttered" with mayonnaise, and Caffeine Free Diet Coke
(or CFDC), appearing like letters of the alphabet, of which none is
superior to any other but which are chosen in accord with the word
we want to spell. For every performer the present is more important
than the past. I pause knowing that no one knows there I am. When
I say "chapter" I mean "train station in Russia," that's what I mean
by the word, and by "word" I mean "huntress" and she means "we
should consider a day lost if we have not danced at least once." Self-
improvement is not the same as personal efficacy, and altruism is
not the same as agency. My husband was currently using a red soft
toothbrush and my wife shaves her legs. Violence in fact almost never
occurs randomly though that any particular instance of it happens
just when and where it does may remain inexplicable. I said that
I knew a man who, recognizing that his wife was undertaking far   *(105*

more of the housework, the shopping, the cooking, and the care of their child than he, calculated the discrepancy in hours and offered her an appropriate monthly salary. A groggy and possibly injured or only drunk man was sprawled just behind the driver of the bus in one of the seats facing the aisle wearing filthy pants that he was now wetting, the urine dripping to the floor, and I was embarrassed, implicated—just as years before, when I was in first grade, after my friend Loretta wet her pants in class and then remained as if caught in her own puddle, I hadn't wanted to go back to school, feeling that I had witnessed something there that I hadn't been meant to see and had thus prematurely acquired forbidden knowledge. But in every situation one anxiously anticipates the possibility that a political correction might be made. The place names in the forty-fourth line of the poem hardly signify. The lack of plot and love of detail should organize my life not according to years or hours but according to spots and stops. Ships. The story seemed plausible, the situation seemed desperate—but then again, due to an emotional naïveté that experience has been unable to shake, I'm inclined to be very gullible. But to remain passive is to engage in ethical mediocrity. Fervors put our thumbs on thistles. That's the point: the emotions provide us with conviction.

We need the language
to aid the senses

We have words to guard continents of fruits and organs. Knowledge is an incitement I turned over. I was in search of a better position, stranger strangers' times. From 10:00 to 1:00, dance one day and draw another; from 1:00 to 2:00 draw on the day you dance and write a letter the day after. My senses too seem to exist—I hear the sounds of a blue jay squawking between the leaves and suddenly again feel the many links between that and the minuscule elements of smell from the gray rain beginning to fall—but the well-known is not necessarily known at all. The moment of panorama, the momentum of preparation. Anticipation is not autonomous. In the dream I was accosted by a woman asking for a mouse with which to distract a great bear that was poised at her feet, growling ferociously, and she warned me not to run for it, she said there'd be no point, bears can travel at forty miles an hour. Well (says someone), we still have the vitality of ourselves in boots from our days on a frontier which we made it our business to contemplate. Rising from behind in the morning, muttering, a phrase plays upon the conquering surface of things. She sang, "I drove my Daddy's Cadillac, from Dallas to the sea, but the prairie holds the cowboy, I'll always want to be." There is no best without its corresponding thing. The rest is discontinuous. The poetry is connection. We are players in a theater of struggling wills. Then write a letter *every* day, though you'll have no guarantee that the communicability of your femininity (or the fact that the substance and mode of your experience *is* communicability) will be admired—it's not you yourself but your life that deserves attention. Destiny must play a part in any good Western, suffusing the landscape with inevitability, itself an expanded frontier, and presenting the moral characters with unavoidable, and often unwelcome, choices. In the dusty town at the Plum Cute Beauty Shop they were offering "shampoos and other passive exercises." The body goes and the head seeks matter. This doesn't lack logic—it is a trick of love. The biggest tree is over there, the man said and pointed, reminding me of the contingency of my expectations. Not form and content but will and content. Just by being under the sky a person knows it exists (and has no need to explain it)—but at this I was interrupted by the smell of smoke, then rising flames, the vastness of which (as well as my inability, after having been told to pack the car to prepare for evacuation, to find anything that seemed worth taking, feeling instead abstracted, severed from both the material and the symbolic orders) subsequently and for many months afterward left me feeling insignificant, insubstantial, and abandoned. I gazed at the cadaver and held its heart, removed from a once melodious cavity. As dislocated as an angel seated on a cloud without ever having had to overcome the forces of gravity. They say that Goethe refused to let his life become "an unstructured and unintended sequence of events," but rather, "each major event in it, foreseen or not, was to be pondered and given its place in a newly interpreted whole." Then compelled to summon strength, to wake up, to get out of bed, and to accept captivity. It was late on Grand Avenue, after 1:00 a.m., the stoplights set only to blink yellow, the four-lane street empty, and I was driving inattentively, until suddenly I was aware that from somewhere, some side street, a cop car had appeared and the guy was flashing his lights at me, flooding me with despair. But I am always shifting scale now. Out of blue rags comes a raging wind rough enough to make a rigid rain. Horses laboring to gallop in the sand, a banjo player in a restaurant moving from table to table. In such autobiographical writings we can trace the effects of mental operations to their source. There is no difference of truth that doesn't make a difference of fact somewhere. The skin moves attention from thing to thing. Emerald Ellie (as she was called, to distinguish her from Ellie Allen, the other Ellie in their "club") was "probably" killed by her boyfriend, Freddy J. (or Jay) Claybridge (aka "Garbage") and "certainly" by repeated hammer blows to the top of her head. The writer realizes her duty to keep the data of what's immediately moving moving. Facts not only are but they are known, and from the time I was old enough to know the facts, remember sounds, require sense, I thought such work had as much similarity to reality as one could provide. Toasting bread, waving the hose, lifting the cat from a chair, I gave myself credit for "joie de vivre." And we've known that—that changing of endlessness, since endlessness is right in front of us. Accuracy is not the voice of nature. The house was clean for its own sake, except for a scrap of paper that I'd missed no bigger than a speck on the floor, and I heaved myself out of the chair and picked up the scrap which, if I'd noticed it a few hours later after the cleanliness had settled, I'd have left. I am not saying that personal generosity will solve everything—it cannot even solve today, not with an act, not with anonymity. Perhaps it's the consummation of all we're going to sadden. The hill is gated, the light has bobbed and dropped, the dog howls, and a rat has torn the door off the oven. The West is confined to infinity. The "philosophical" (i.e., resigned) cattle turn their heads to look at us as we hike by and swarming from a small mound at the side of the road there are ants (they are social but do not pretend to come from any country). According to Tolstoi's Yardstick, humans get their ideas from words but horses get them from facts. I still, now and then, see Madame on the street, an elegant though tiny and now very old woman carrying a small bundle of groceries in a string bag, but I don't speak to her, out of shyness and the near certainty that she wouldn't remember me, whom she "had" in her fifth-grade French class almost forty years ago, but also out of terror, since she taught her class with such ferocity, expressing, I suppose, passionate belief in the rightness, the superiority, the perfection of *pied* over *foot*, and *mont* over *hill*, that she made my life miserable, until one evening, as I was riding to my grandparents' house in the little township in the Oakland hills called Piedmont, I felt the sudden triumphant pleasure that comes from linking one thing to another, the thrill of making sense. We live in a relative state, with prepositional sensations. At the live porn theater I was to see that each woman paradoxically hid her mound by shaving it. On a chair at night in old clothes at my desk beside the window looking out during a storm at the wind pouring over the trees under the streetlight. The schizophrenic, gazing at something, watches it turn not only unfamiliar but unreal, but the artistic gaze (and the resulting defamiliarization) heightens a thing's palpability, sees it turn not only unfamiliar but real. There is altruism in poetry. Come morning the wind in the sunlight is the color of spilling milk. But the hills are charred, houses lost, and the city stretches out, named for Bishop George Berkeley, in honor of his line, "Westward the course of empire takes its way." The knowledge is embodied—and the body is trembling, terrified, because it's unprepared, it forgot to get ready, it forgot to buy food, it forgot to dress. And so to believe it to be what we truly believe it to be we must open it. In words to have my moments twice, I writhe. It finds itself (or, more precisely, cannot find itself, and advances) staring at itself. The West is here—we can ground our uncertainties on nothing else.

We think of these,
the polar circles

I ask myself, "What's in a poem." These are places where the action never stops. The outside of the world—but this itself is that. Looking after, being ready before. Tendrils, I said, but my sister heard ten girls: ten girls in the ferns. Within those two weeks of summer, one in the Colorado mountains and one near the North Sea, I met three different women, each of them living by careful design far from cities and alone, and I took these meetings as an omen. Across in a kayak from Afognak to Kanatak with the mannish Mrs. Feather and the mannish Mrs. Farmer—every form of association is possible. The sentence is a logical form regardless of the matter. I remember even as a child realizing that pleasure lay in arranging it. A storm came in—blue-black clouds and wind—and I was excited by it, or by the anticipation of something else of which it was the gust. A shock, and I wanted to be as impersonal as it. I would take a solid seat and see. I would take the first four trees I came to, give them a day each, drawing them leaf by leaf, branch by branch, and even twig by twig as carefully as if they were rivers and the page an important map. The travelogue is not a foray into exoticism but an account of its author's most petty problems (and most banal achievements). It seemed that we had never begun and we would never be there. I imagined the austere inevitable stillness of the Arctic pole. Doing "nothing"—nothing having no connection with anything, being a name without a referent, an unlinked phrase—it coincides only with itself, generating no surplus, no grounds for meaning something. It bears no relation to the marvel that is Hamlet's father's ghost, the body of a disembodied parent, who does indeed exist now even if only in the form of one who existed previously, so that one must speak of him now in a strange grammar, as one who exists some time ago, one now who exists then. *(111*

I was embarrassed by the glare, or by my watering eyes, and as I looked at my friend her image weakened and the world closed in until I rose "in blind panic" overcome by claustrophobia from the swirling white table that had become indistinguishable from the sun. Horses pounce, no comma. Forget-me-nots his favorite flower: his rigors were always local. I was a year older now than my father had ever been, a year older, too, than the grandmother I "took after." It is we who are ominous; the future promises nothing. I studied the famous painting called "Sailors Rescue Women from Drowning"—in the foreground a woman floats, her face suffused by an ice-blue gray pallor, and behind her other women are being rescued by sailors who are in the ocean with them, while on shore other sailors are bathing rescued women, wiping the pallor from their faces, which are now round and healthy, though some residue of white remains around their ears like shaving cream. We know "tomorrow we will be here," and "every person has its double" to demand more logics from life. Reason looks for two and arranges it from there. And it wasn't so much hopelessness as a sense of lessening obligation that made me think I too could die, dead before, dead after, but alive now as I say so. Northern stories always revolve around meetings with natural spirits and the problem of how to treat them well so as to receive their aid, while ours are filled with the boisterous dead, the restless guilty, implacable ghosts. And already in Cooper, especially in *The Pioneers*, American remorse serves to embolden nostalgia, and human flamboyance is sheltered by the ghosts of trees. The river, clear and amber, like tea from peat, ran deep through the bear circle in the forest. Mineral always turns animal in the machines it symbolizes. Sometimes the will inspects the goodness of being and remains passive before it. In a socket of earth it burns. There are hunters there, all of them conservationists, and some tension develops because no one is sure who should take on the role of hostess to provide coherence to the occasion. Parataxis is characteristic of atheism as of polytheism, but while the parataxis of polytheism is limitless that of atheism is unbound. My students that spring didn't know how to talk in class, since what they could talk about—what they did—wasn't what one "studied" in schools—having the saturating experiences of music, shopping, "hanging," TV. They were having the subjectivity of consumers, lacking objectivity amid abundant objects. The grasses waggled, obvious ballads, dreams. An enormous man crashed through the drugstore's plate-glass window, there was considerable commotion, but apart from a small cut on his arm on which the pharmacist put a dab of Neosporin and a Band-Aid, he wasn't hurt, the incident had been brought on entirely by allergies, he said, but they were "much" to his "embarrassment." Whatever the subject, the man said—feminism, thinking, individualism, sex, writing, science, etc.—sooner or later I perceive the inevitable approach of the topic with which Americans are most obsessed, that of their own violence. In one show, nature (the ocean) has polluted culture (the hero), he's contracted hepatitis from bacteria thriving in the surf around a supposedly unused sewage outlet that in fact has been spewing untreated effluent, the waves can be seen surging in the background as he says to the woman doctor who has come to warn him away from the beach, "When a big wave appears, I've always got to ride her." He was at Two Rivers and saw a woman standing on her head. The malice of earth? Its solace. Who are wanderers? Today's brightest spots are void, and indeed it seems as if I have to will all of all these days into memory, as if memory, which had a will of its own during childhood, was now reluctant to attend to the day, or as if the light accumulated by time was overpowering the details around us, the way sunlight blazing on a page obliterates the type. The sun has sealed the sea. I would write so I myself could see if what I'd written was right. An analysis of details alternates with scenes, and there are pauses for these analyses, themselves scenes. It is a work of moments inserted. And especially for love—because time entails inescapability. Along the border between fields of sunflowers turning, where only two years earlier guards had been posted to keep people in, now guards from the other side were posted to keep them out. We rowed out on the lake to the island in the midnight light, the water dark, cold, smooth, glowing. We stood on the deck in the Arctic looking north—a work of links and circles. We hiked through the pastel air over the tundra, mosquitoes leapt, lighter and lighter, more and more happy, on into the pale night at the edge of which the sun floated. Why not remember sleeps as well as dreams. Why not write with unbounded identity and geographical fluidity. Sentence by sentence, all these exertions (looping, jutting, and providing pleasure from numerous sources), these judgments and extensions, whose curves often repeat themselves, form a whole which, despite momentary pauses, is unbroken by the angles, shadows, and impeding particles included. But years are not pauses, not roses, and who, I asked, was the nation's president the year Herman Melville wrote *Moby-Dick*. I don't remember, someone says, but she means she does not know, she feels no gap haunted by the rhythm of a name she can't quite say, the want she feels isn't supplied with a name but instead is a wanting to know, so she looks it up, next time I'll remember, she vows, but a year later she didn't. There is no deeper secret to immortality than having lived.

And of these,
the binding moments

I stood long at the gate watching cows in tranquility. One by one in a heterogeneity, two by two in a plenitude. I stood at the window watching skateboarding boys propel themselves through the parking lot, up the makeshift plank ramp, and over three cardboard boxes placed end to end in a calm. We perceive nothing but relationships—perception itself is that. She was developing a rock garden in the woods, cultivating ferns, wildflowers, and miniature evergreens. My sleeps are the vivid confines of my mind. Little was left but the indentation. The road to Angkor Wat was mined. She hated to change rotations, to feel like a foreigner lost between wards. Vowing to alleviate suffering is not the same as anticipating a world without it. Early this morning I observed that after first light there's a second dark, and it's out of that second dark that the true light of day appears. The family gathered around the kava with continuity. I had wanted to be the doctor, but it had been the situation of the patient that most fascinated me, as if the one thing certain was the inadequacy of prior solutions and the one thing to be achieved was the reappraisal of possibility. My attorney lifts the tortilla from the burner, sprigs of mint garnish the platter. It's an oddity of U.S. law that a person cannot be required to incriminate him or herself verbally but may be required to do so physically (by appearing in a lineup, for example). The face of the cadaver was still intact and it had a pensive countenance. Immobility creates a profuse focal point, so that if we linger we blur. The pressure of the tongue must be firm, the release must be abrupt and clean-cut, and worry as well will take some of the sense out. So we feel but do not see humanity. I eased the artery from the gray meat of the groin. I'll accept the risk that's incurred when one volunteers for doubt. While traveling (and we insist on motion) we shift the center of gravity and with it the nature of confinements. Then progress (according to the research clock) changes the look of things and with it the value of things. Love indeed conjectures love. Ships cleaving to the waves cleave the sea famously. Overhead inland a mosquito rings like a spinning belt. This is the year that culture is conjectured in Antwerp. Even this, said the man pointing to the stage — even this is a site of class struggle, embodied in competing linguistic nationalisms, and the result can be crazy and make organizing cultural events unpleasant, so we do it in English. Over and over the small research vessel climbed the north face of the eighty-foot wave and fell to the valley south of it. A damp wind lashed the awning of the cafe, no shadows fell on the cobblestoned square. What *is* the nature of this strange work — but it has no nature, only condition. Dense, animate music, an encircling circle, secret, Magritte. I thought I saw a nurse in white aloft on a potato, but then I saw it was a swan eating a tomato. If it's metempsychotic it's Sisyphean. We would speak twice of what we see, we would agree and disagree. But for the Hopi (according to Benjamin Lee Whorf in "The Relation of Habitual Thought and Behavior to Language" which I'd read years before, had largely forgotten, and was now reading again), the word "day" has no plural form, since there has always only been one day, this one, departing with the dark and returning with the light, eternally collecting experience; "to the Hopi, for whom time is not a motion but a 'getting later' of everything that has ever been done, unvarying repetition is not wasted but accumulated." I see a large field of "carrots" — these are slender auburn animals resembling elk and they are browsing in the grass. A private investigator needs to be able to catch the telling phrase, as when the client's brother says he has "no regrets" about their childhood because "there wasn't anything wrong with it." He'd been the only man at the conference not carrying a gun, and while the others stood around the resort's swimming pool in the heat of the mid-afternoon sun with their "pieces" poorly concealed under their untucked short-sleeved shirts, he dove into the water and swam about, he "had the pool all to himself." There's a critical difference between calling the course "The Harlem Renaissance" and calling it "Reading the Harlem Renaissance" and for me the latter was the wiser course. I am compiling an assortment of scientific anecdotes, each one filling about half a large sheet of gridded blue paper. Beginning from the body, a moving thing, we perceive. He felt he didn't "get anything" from high school but supposed the value of high school is that it "keeps you out of trouble." I like an answering voice at last light that says carry on, wagging the shadow of which you are the premonition. It's unlikely I'd attribute malice to that. I found myself following Fall Creek and thinking up courses, skies without "sameness," perhaps something called "1899" in which we'd read Winston Churchill's *Richard Carvel*, Charles Chesnutt's *Wife of His Youth and Other Stories of the Color Line*, Edwin Markham's "Man with the Hoe," Elbert Hubbard's *Message to Garcia*, Paul Lawrence Dunbar's *Lyrics of the Hearthside*, Henry James's *The Awkward Age*, Kate Chopin's *The Awakening*, Jack London's "To Build a Fire," Booker T. Washington's *The Future of the American Negro*, William James's *Talks to Teachers on Psychology: and to Students on Some of Life's Ideals*, and Ambrose Bierce's *Fantastic Fables*. The artist doesn't paint clouds she paints time, she paints with the eye of enduring. The sentence, an island only temporarily and tentatively colonized, sails, an aphorism on a page painted by a stranger. This has little to do with immigration law, though there too there is a hero. We wade past (the minnows are ugly swollen things) and get on the boat. I am enraged—I think of jumping into the pool to fight—I want to punch the girl in the face. We were at the market but not at the one that was at 3000. He remembered a picnic at which the adults "were drinking" and his father had called his uncle "a fat slob," the uncle had told his father "to put your money where your mouth is," and the uncle challenged the father to a foot race, which the uncle "at 300 and some odd pounds" won. The warping of the floorboards under the kitchen linoleum must be the result of a long-term leak, and I'd guess that the delightful women plumbers two years ago put the pipes in wrong. Who was the president that year? Some kind of consciousness is always going on. One begins as a student but becomes a friend of clouds. Please note that in my attempt to increase the accuracy of these sentences and the persistence and velocity with which they proceed, I'm pursuing change while trying to outrun the change that's pursuing me. Consciousness carries us farther and farther into the world. Perhaps will and fate are the same chance.

Intention provides
the field for inquiry
and improvisation the
means for inquiring

Fences marginalize a cowboy. Let there be sentences—circular sentences; sentences incorporating pauses, roses. Life will add thickness ("the thickness of time"). It provides us with the potential for forming the relationship between our curious subjectivity and every fascinating thing. We are hurled to imagine ourselves hurling and we hurl together. One night I had the dream of "The Three Sisters and the Hangman's Hut" and another night I dreamed of "The Moral Trespasser and the Fair-minded Spring." Where are we?—"in a series," to quote Emerson, "of which we do not know the extremes." Shall we do some ungendering, shall we gently cross-dress. The fingers aren't stiff, but they weaken, forefinger especially feeling floppy, quivering, losing accuracy, distracted by a rhythm, like that of a train passing in the early morning hours blowing its whistle. There have been "developments," things are "dramatic." Despite a growing sensitivity to social life guiding my attention, I began to laugh—a slight revolt—for which I immediately apologized. In and as this. It's all just a worrying after the control that would get one to that perfect point at which it's all departure, all glimpsed, all discussed, our desire desiring itself at the moment that expectations are relaxed, in a quirky deepening of companionship, in the quirky depths of companionship. I walked a straight mile and then a crooked one to campus, passing from bright light into gloom and from gloom into bright light moodily but doggedly. Always when experimenting, one must be neither shy nor certain. Facticity consists in being at origin (speaking here not of the original how but of the original why) inexplicable (a fact has original inexplicability: that's a fact, bingo! no fact is flat). But we need the language to aid the senses, and it all begins wonderfully on page 82, first word. Every word   *(119* is an experience in the genre of the gentle exchange. Once upon a time, far away and long ago, though not all that long ago, sometime after the world began but before you were born—I can't be more precise—what do you think I am, a clock? Yes, events tend to cluster along the chronological line. I dream of a hero who is able to toss animals from a great distance. Permanent revolution, ongoing life. Our lachrymose dinner guest sighed again wiping tears from his eyes and continued to lament the death of the "noble poor bear," last survivor of the zoo in Sarajevo. But an imaginary world of vast possibility is an inadequate utopia, while an achieved utopia is an unacceptable possibility. To be born at all seems chancy, and having been born, that it should have happened now and here and in human form to me even more so, but after that the most remarkable things occur at points of forced encounter between facts of equal strange-ness. I've done everything I'm supposed to do, washed my face, I plan my days, then I paid too close attention to the words on the page, noted the points at which, after offering only quick glimpses, they each departed from the ideas they were meant to convey, but the ideas themselves had already escaped me, and I thought I'd say all this (all that) to Larry, wondered at the desire to do so, the wis-dom of the desire, the wonder of acting on desire, a life of reason in this deracinated condition, talking to people I'll never know better. A thousand thoughts and one thought. We must sleep for pressure, sleep for sprawl. The numerous ill lay laughing, several to a bed. The canny look on this occasion was an uncanny one, they saw from the site of secrets. On the sidewalk at the window outside the restaurant in the "ever-widening gap" between themselves and the rich stood a crowd. This is all familiar: Henry teases Jane, Jane intrigues Cassie, William shares Willa's enthusiasm for Charles Dickens. The poems (as you, curiously, didn't seem to have noticed) were on a variety of different kinds and sizes of paper, some on enormous index cards, some bound into sets of miniature books, some inscribed on maps, so it was not a manuscript but an exhibition, the meditation embodied by the work (or works) having been made exterior and public; the work was performance. The coward replaces a public dilemma (demanding intervention, objection, argument) with a private one (her cowardice). There were two of them suddenly on the ice, tails up and sauntering, paying us "no mind." I was on an empty road in an Italian town in front of a yellow villa, having come a long way in a black carriage to visit Flaubert. From here on the plot will involve a conflict between secrets and sequences. I was passing a church on a warm Tuesday morning as the organist (I assumed) was practicing or just testing the pipes in canyons of blue timber. She had "the greatest confidence in everything" which gave her a tendency to amiability, coherence, until she found that she had gotten along and gone along and now was "in a frenzy." My mother was singing in the ship's rigging. The waves were hurled apart. Later the Ranger confirmed that those were wolves. Am I willfully disinterested, you ask, am I complacent—no, I'm thoroughly pissed off. I "talk to myself" and *as* myself, too, not yet knowing what I myself (or, better, selves) will say, what the rules are and will become, first thought flowing in imitation of a previous thought of a previous self one could say with equal accuracy scrawling or sprawling without limit, and yet that's not right. On some other occasion, I may visit Cézanne! Let us thrill to the intellectual, moral, and aesthetic emotions. Visiting my mother's and stepfather's house in New Hampshire, I took great pleasure in seeking "great treasure" in the soil under the trees that had grown up in and around the site of a 100-year-old trash pit—shards of pottery, rusty springs and nails, old buttons, and occasionally unbroken bottles with long and narrow necks, though by far the bulk of what I turned up with my little trowel was broken glass. Meanwhile self-sufficient wild animals in great numbers (elk, eagles, bears, wolves, mosquitoes, midges, butterflies, deer, woodpeckers, etc.) live spread out to the north, each allocated to an environment appropriate to its needs, and each, adapting its belief to the evidence, sure that where it lives is "right." There are no unequal facts, I was beginning to say. They sat along three walls of the room, the middle of which was all windows, and I, their sole audience, sat facing into the light, blinded, unable to see their faces, so that I was forced to turn inward, to plunge into my role, at which they, my audience, gazed. It all lasted just about as long as a play, and then we went to a cafe, which is where I really learned something. We were not at the margin but on the border, mind lost in body, skirt over our head. Scheherazade told her instructive tales to the governor and after that he governed better. You should enthuse over that, not this. When one apologizes or fringes one's statements with disclaimers, one gives one's auditors power but also binds them to one—they are now responsible for one's shortcomings, burdened with one's inadequacies. The self is a site of time absorbing dissonances. I find that I don't really mind that the cheering at the outdoor concert escapes the site and can be heard for several miles around in the summer night. There is no simple organic link between two instants, instead one must make "a pathetic jump," passing from the first into the next, passing the power of the first to the second. But more of that another time. The writing moved sense and made it.

I could count to zero   Every word has a staking effect. What
is the meaning hung from that suspend.
Between during along including and all
along. In the "Pedagogical" notebook
under "Poetry and Ethics" in the section
labeled "the limitless, the impasse, the
border, chance," I find a notion credited
to Deleuze, who says all that ethics requires is that we not be unworthy of what happens to us. The narrative returns from a journey to
the pole but the narrator is left behind. There's no stop, just rope and
drift, loop and tug. I was listening to the ornithologically ambiguous
sounds of horns, I masked my disappointment that we didn't pull
over to look at the sea. I am no Robinson Crusoe. I wanted to defend
description, to elaborate on both the pleasure and the information to
be found both in describing and in being described to, but the awareness, which came to me even as I was formulating my defense, that
the third possibility, that of being described, I would hate, made me
doubt my previous enthusiasm, though it occurred to me, too, that,
though I wouldn't like to have people view me, see me, scrutinize me,
I wouldn't for that reason condemn eyes, scrutiny, or sight. The head
is at the hill where it so loves the view of the hill flowing on awhile.
Here is the difference between objective and subjective, said Leslie
Scalapino: one can make an objective statement about anything one
can make a statement about; the subjective is that realm about which
one can't say anything at all. One old woman coughs up a sapphire,
the other blows an emerald from her nose. In war each side tries to
convince its audience of the supreme value of what it stands to lose.
Cast in Waterford crystal, the life-size replica of Bear Bryant's hat
sat under spotlights on a slowly turning pedestal throwing bright
reflections out into the room while the fight song blared. They called
it "swayt tay" and I left it in its sweating glass sitting on the table.   *(123*

It's the all-consuming consuming all. It is all about old boys and they are all about football. Around the periphery of the field, just outside the fence, runs a shallow ditch lined with hard plastic, into which, when ant collectors stir up the horses in the field until they are rearing and bucking and pawing and dashing about, the thunder of hooves drives thousands of ants. If one (being gullible, credulous) is to teach herself skepticism, she must resist the urge to provide explanations. The *non sequitur* is something (which does not follow), the *nihil sequitur* is nothing (which follows). Things are all causes and their ever-changing interconnection is what we term destiny. Lightning danced over the Delta as we turned onto a muddy track and came in sight of the river flowing past an industrial site under a wide dark stone and steel bridge beneath which in deep shadow three white men sat in a rowboat fishing. It was with skepticism (more than irony) that I called the Mississippi mug that I bought at a shop just across the border my "freedom cup." I could call it fixation, embassy, convenience, or hyperbole. By negativity, I mean our interest in, even obsession with, the unknown, the meaningless, the unspeakable, the unapproachable, the unbearable, the impasse; by sublimity, I mean recognition of "the gap" and the ecstasy (with its concomitant sense of doubleness, sense of wonder, sense of awe, sense of alienation) that one feels in the face of the unspeakable; by affirmation, I mean a commitment to opening that gap in order to make room for new possibilities, multifaceted generosities, tolerance, the giving and receiving of pleasure. All the more costly (and yet, as we'll see, also all the more mostly). Doubt is a form of accusation, a putting under suspicion (since, if the subject is proven to be truly dubious, it will be discredited and condemned to irrelevance), but doubt in that case might serve as a release—leaving one to turn away, setting the issue aside with only one last shrug. And regrets?—regrets regard and some charge. One day the princess stepped across a stream, took up her binoculars, and spotted a flock of tiny birds, but the light was wrong and they flew away, and whether they were chickadees or bushtits she was never sure, although the word "no" had never meant anything to her. It is just as Hannah Arendt says, "Though history ultimately becomes the storybook of mankind, no one's life has an author." Mystics, Arkadii responded, have access to nothing through memory in flashes of their non-being. Yes. That there's the father of all waters, said the drunk man on the log, to which the sober man standing on the sand replied, then that must be the Mistersippi. Out in the country about an hour farther south was the Sin Garden of a remorseful man. According to Goya, the sleep of reason brings forth monsters. It was my inclination, my desire, to be interested and thus to be pleased—to be "getting something out of" the situation—but instead of interest I felt horror. With the threat of death, the promise of death, there may come a sense of sudden freedom, but only for the dying, while for her friends and family her dying produces a sense of restriction, of limit, since, while the dying person will go onward, will "pass away," the living must remain behind, like prisoners. She tucked her pinky under her thumb and pointed her three middle fingers to the left to indicate that I was exaggerating. Large leashed lumpy dogs appeared one night in my dreams and they all pulled in different directions against these connections. The memory of that dream is now a mere abbreviation. I'm in a tent pitched on a slope looking west with my two cats, now as big as panthers, and a female lion, who has befriended us—or should I say "taken our side" in "another wild kingdom"? Who could argue that selves are pillars alone. Our souls are our copies, they ignore us completely. I interrupt, not to seize power (though, in a sense, I do so) but to participate, corroborate, collaborate. Of course it is pointless to say something that can't be understood, and yet, though you cannot understand my love for you, it is not pointless to tell you of it. Leaves are being blown through the open casement window, itself swinging, and with the leaves comes a moth, a sphinx. I pass from one genre to the next day, a seat of different sensations. There once was a beautiful princess whose favorite color was red and she lived in a dark forest where only the tiniest flowers grew and they were yellow. The molten metal cooled and was beaten into brittle rattles, while the little children prattled to the kitten and the rattlesnake battled with a turtle. Michael interrupted to say that his friend Ben considered vinyl far superior to CDs, and Rae cracked, "Hurray for crackle." Sleep receiver of words. In social stages we make our way adjusting to dreams at break of day disguising as fun our ineptitude as we're seized by untested solicitude. I looked closely at the photos of the faces of the frozen men, their lips drawn back, not to grimace or snarl but as if they were weeping. Waking phrases come unwanted, unwarranted: I am afraid not of their sound (though it's malignant) but of their banality, their illogicality. They are unfinished night thoughts, uncut sweeps, unchanted gears. Haphazard discernments. No. In what way. In this way. Life makes zero mandatory, life makes zero nearly impossible.

This is a hazard of happiness

This is happening. This is an homage to Flaubert. There was once a princess who was turned into a salmon and then turned out of it again. Words negate nothing—but this proposition is false, since if words negate nothing (i.e., don't negate), they cannot negate nothing (i.e., negate). A word to guard continents of fruits and organs. It is a writing of reasons. It is a politics, a chance. If we received our fate at birth, then the question one would have to ask of a child is how will she behave while she awaits her fate. I am sent to Room 117, but I can't find it—I am told that it exists but it is in "the double world" to which my doppelganger has already departed, and, that being the case, I am already there. It was easy to pass between the barriers that had been set up—I just turned sideways and wiggled (everyone I passed averted their eyes). Animals seemed to have lost their fear, a wild rabbit approached, a hummingbird hovered nearby, the garden towhees had become familiars. Where there are borders there is barbarism. Then the gypsy's goose jumped onto the bed and pecked at my thighs until all the ants were gone. This created a clinical situation, turned for speculation. Under itself is the buried equator—but philosophers at a lake always think of going under. I would write nothing—the counting to zero, the stepping backward to the pole. Bug best because best belief becomes best. A run and if I broke it I'd have none. I stood at the xerox machine with a bandage under my eye hidden by my dark glasses ready to provide "on demand" an explanatory anecdote, pointless, why explain, baby, just say good-bye. The vultures swooped, flying so close that I could hear the fluttering of their feathers and the strange sound they uttered, more clack than call, a rattling like that of large seeds in a can. Fleeting charges of power, species, season, shape, race, location, gender. *Multum in parva*—a little russet pebble; *multum in nihilo*—that produces practitioners. And here is a woman in whom a second-grade teacher discerned a talent for math. Service rushes seclusion, seclusion raises service. I pulled down the textbook on entomology. An actual thing does seem in some way to be the cause of this statement's being true. But increasing signs of dreams have appeared—they have shuffled forward, following the woman in the still bulk of her chair to whom so many pauses occur that she must count continually forward and then back or else she'll be surpassed. The speakers would shift, giving way to speakers within and to speakers within that. Fate never fails. Now almost 100, the old woman, in her near total deafness, was able nonetheless to greet and exchange extensive pleasantries with all her visitors, knowing from long habit a full stock of phrases and where they should fall and prepared also with compliments such as "it's lovely to see you" or "how nice you look," which might fall anywhere. Their smiles stretched wearily across her face. I buried the blameless bundle of hair. I lovingly took the head in my lap but it lay upside down and looked like that of a cyclops with an *ocula dentata*. We know people by what they do, yes, but also by what happens to them. A cowboy will want to be known as that as he waves his hat to think a real individual is created in visibility. Response: aphorisms are fatuous. I blurted out the secret and gazed at the ghost of having told it. Having been told by my sister that my nephew wants to get his college degree in history, I spoke to him with an enthusiasm I knew to be "contagious" of the infinite re-(or pro-?)gression that constitutes the interpretations we call "history," interpretations which themselves each have a history, which in turn—but No! he interrupted, don't tell me that! throughout my entire childhood I've been *terrified* of infinity! and that's why I've always wanted to study history—it's

limited, to the past! so don't start telling me the past is infinite! That forest with the creek falling through it now has the status of a state park and the old ghost town at the end of the five-mile trail that of an abandoned museum. I could fill notebooks with things interpreted differently, I could puke. No, we were not sinking. The sea is hard. We are warned against the thorns of the compass and the sun so we are prepared. Hightailing it toward the sunset with the sun in my eyes I came all over goose bumps. I found the birds ominous, but the omen was good. We stay in and on the evidence. I'd been sure that the talk, no matter the degree of animation, no matter the force of our agreements or disagreements, was all intended for the general good. But it's been hot, or rather the weather has intensified, becoming concentrated, so that people sweat as if sensing peril. The strangers participate in events, some of which last no more than a second and some of which have been unfolding for years. A pause, a glance, a rose, a knitted hat, the passing by of a passerby: something on paper. They had been bigots, they had called my father Pinko. A turbulent dispersion of ink in water drawn by fountains to the inside of my world. It is hard to turn away from moving water, the beneficial bonfire in which you burned the clothes. Creating mean-ingfulness for the meanings this conveys *is* its meaningfulness. The whole barnyard. Your Willie to my Winnie was so convincing that alarmed nurses rushed in. I thought I saw a crumpled blanket ly-ing on the bed, but then I saw it was an improviser standing on his head. What lives in the grave are bones and reputation, what dies is experience. This happened in the blink of an eye, but ever after the princess remembered the river—its dappled shadows, the weaving of currents of warm water through the cold, the slowly tumbling rocks in the rills over the shallows. All of it, if you've got the time.

Along comes something,   That's an affirmative. And yet we have
launched in context   the pessimism to crave. Article adjective
                              adjective noun verb preposition pronoun
                              noun comma pronoun noun dash gerund
                              copula preposition article noun. Now
                              compare that sentence of last night to this
                              morning's sentence addressed to you, in

and out of the house and I can't decide about the movie either, but
really I think it would depress me—the color, the plot, the end. For
a spider to move from the center of the web toward a stimulus in
the web, the spider needs conviction. Anaximander observes (or so
Karl Jaspers says), that "once the world has come into being, guilt
is no doubt an inevitable consequence of its antagonisms." Reason
looks for three. Can this counter corporation. The explorers moved
in the course of empire, the horizon widened what it cost them. Kings
playing chess on fine green sand. But—though, strictly speaking,
observation cannot demonstrate this, since, though they are, they
can only (though they must) be supposed—large parts of the day
refuse to come forward, and, if they deposit themselves anywhere
at all, it is certainly not in our minds, we are dispossessed of them,
and they will never belong to us. I wake with emotion, but what if
the emotions are not "triggered," what if they are not responses but
capable of rising independently, as pure affect. A human, too, is a
"thing in itself" to itself. Character, stray convenience, the laugh, the
catch. The focus of one's work may lie somewhere other than where
one thinks one is focusing. It seems from our methodical and even
obsessive habits of attention, though they are far inferior to those
of the patient and meticulous empiricists who year after year first
measured the course and ever-changing relative positions of the stars,
that we continue to maintain a belief that the advance of the hour or
day (or, for some, even of the year) entails its coming to mind and

that the aggregate, the accumulation of arrivals in consciousness (like that of fruit flies to a rotting peach) will add up to our knowing, at the very least, just what our life has consisted of. Obscure. As Gertrude Stein's one-time mentor William James observed, this is "where things happen": "reality, life, experience, concreteness, immediacy, use what word you will, exceeds our logic, overflows and surrounds it . . . —and by reality here I mean where things *happen*." If then whenever nonetheless worldly—because worldly. The photographer is depicted as a young man hurling thunderbolts in the bards' circle, the cluster of cows couched in the dew at dawn strikes a dolorous chord, and the shoemaker, having suffered a heart attack, closes his shop. One wants one's work to be shareable—one seeks the shareable (*not* the universal). The entomologist, as she herself says, can tell you everything she knows about ants but nothing as to what ants know about themselves. It's a space of appearance, a space of dilemma. Parallelisms—one has to follow one's parallelisms. The deep blue paint around the doors of the house is meant to ward off evil, and if it can't do it all, the statue of the Virgin of Guadalupe is meant to do the rest. Two stunning men dressed in black and wearing brown vests whom I took to be gypsies were singing and playing their guitars at the Spring Street station, twins who were, as far as I could see, absolutely identical, except that one was a tenor and the other a baritone, their two voices playing off each other brilliantly, and I let several trains go by, which is why I was late. An event is an adventure of the moment. A man a woman arrives from the East the West bringing taking a summons dismissal that I am sending following and my confusion is clear unclear. The apples rotting in the grass below scented the dust which two hovering bees very slightly stirred before darting off as I descended. Intention provides the field for inquiry, improvisation is the mode of inquiring. You can see where a coyote crossed a tile. All that occurs does so in many ways. But bigotry is almost always devoted to enforcing separation and sustaining separateness. Flash's party discovers that Ming's scientist has perfected death dust so that it will only kill people of high intelligence. Doubt seizes — it grasps at the very things it doubts. I'm an internationalist then, i.e., an antinationalist — yes. When confronted with the challenge of judging the ethicality of another person's actions, it is best to assume that the situation in which they occurred was complicated. Things, being perceived, produce my reasons. There are an infinite number of sequences underway. My grandmother vowed to learn a new word every day and never at this age be ashamed to dance. The secret, she said, was in the pomegranate seeds lacing the salad with aphrodisia. Some of the lines in this family saga must be inscribed in Spanish. Here's a "situation" for a novel: a passionate woman finds herself so humiliated by the effects of age that she can hardly bear to go out, she feels disgraced, she is appropriate to no situation, she decides to found a theater company. This sign of art, this single indication, is marking a site at which at some other time some other human lived and thought. Two years later I will rise early and patiently await the changing state of my being complicitous with my fate. Hold this position for a part of a second, then release the pressure quickly by removing the tongue from the gums, deftly. The realm of the incoherent yields a profusion of fruits. The novel will conjure up a family I never had. I remember that I sat in the apple tree and ate a Gravenstein, still cool with life from the tree in the hot summer afternoon sun. It would be like this one, replete with unfathomable discrepancies. Three eggs and a corn tortilla — imaginary objects. Then the feral cats that Senora Paz feeds next door come over the wall at night and shit at her feet. There's only one antidote to the dust — polarite. It is inaccurate to say that he who cannot love turns up frequently but remains unloved. Who we are — it is only partly revealed in the patterns of our lives — something remains hidden in our intentions. We take the great parts of a human life to be distinct, far more so than the transitions that oppose and distinguish them, but childhood and adulthood, youth and age, are never juxtaposed, unless perhaps in spaces like those that lie between the frames of a film — and it was in just such a space that the dancing at the wedding began. For experimentation here augment, insert, extend. The members of the mariachi band, somber as always, were waiting just outside the mission doors. One must sustain the value of the real world — it must be valued — when it is devalued it ceases to compel recognition. There has always only been one day, and with it we are developing a lifelong relationship.

From the first moment I saw this I wanted to write on it. And strange as it may seem, the resulting story interests me not because it proceeds toward an end but because what proceeds works backward toward a beginning and begins. I'm *still* an existentialist. "Existence precedes essence": we make our appearance and then define ourselves. Existing never to non-exist again. We knew he'd be a boy, and we rocked in anticipation, waiting for him to figure out. Even as an infant, he broods bravely. Listening to the wind in the trees I heard sounds which seemed to have had their origins, if not in another galaxy then at least in the idea of other galaxies whose remoteness was not just geophysical or astronomical but emotional, and I wanted to know more of it—I lifted my head off the pillow against which my ear had been muffled and opened my eyes. Augustine notes this moment and says, "I have become a question to myself." It's a lyric shuttle or a carpenter's kettle, and we can make it mutable. The real are the active ingredients of a metamorphosis. Here is a thought, no longer mine, and I called it *amor fati*. The politician binds his thinking to results; the poet must renounce results and continue thinking. But real referring is worthy of respect. It used to be that one referred to "so-called language writing," but it's time to omit the "so-called" (or to regard it as a so-called "so-called"). Meanings are nothing but a flow of contexts—names trimmed with colored ribbons. But those who favor the material, contingent, or *a posteriori* features of the world are generally labeled empiricists. The world is what I'm made of, but the world is not made of me—it was already there, it will be there afterward, what is it. Too many questions. Perhaps one records one's moods ("June 26: gloomy, irritable—as if grieving" or "July 5: excited, restless—distracted by potential happiness [but perhaps happiness and potentiality are the same thing?]") not out of narcissism but in the hope that they may prove a register, indicative not only of the state of one's psyche but also of the state of the world. This moment exists in two temporalities, it exists always and briefly. It is time itself, particularly since the shift from a product to a service economy, that is being asked to yield increasing amounts of wealth. Many times upon a time there lived a bird who laid a figure on a twisted bough and invited a spider to help her raise it. They called the great rock Aphrodite. A single African flower appeared on my father's grave—unanticipated but not by chance. A windmill doesn't come to a location however but rather a location comes into existence because of a windmill perhaps a bridge. But what of the trapper adopted by the Pomo and given the name of Never Mind. The being at a loss. At the site of the pass into the postmodern infinity called the border I sat intransigently, laughing. He needed only hot water, as he had his own tea. If I were to decide to insert into this book—as much an exhibition of reappearances as an autobiography, since the self it "expresses," existing only in and as writing, and with that writing broken into sentences, changes place and even disappears behind the familiar—photographs, they might impede or even arrest the "developments" on which the meaningfulness (the acknowledging of the familiar's reappearances) depends. Others want to go into the basement but that doesn't seem logical – why would the basement be safer. As we were walking on the beach we were joined by a shorthaired mottled brown male dog who seemed to feel fond of us, looking back if it got ahead to make certain we were following or running to catch up with us if it fell behind, and then suddenly it left us. As William James says, "The idea of chance is, at bottom, exactly the same thing as the idea of gift . . . [a] name for anything on which we have no effective *claim*." Commas between the penultimate and ultimate of a series, question mark mid-sentence, yes, but let tone determine emphasis, and let tone determine query at sentence's end. There are ironies between aphorisms—traces of sensibility. I was "seething" with irritation, and the irritant was myself, or, rather, the irritation, since what had provoked it (a mess and the picking up that eliminated it, carried out in a kind of hurry, even frenzy, brooking no interruption, no pause, as if it had to be carried out against a deadline) was gone, and I wondered what had caused the initial sense of hurry, since, though I recognized that the cleaning up of the mess (unwashed dishes, sections of the newspaper strewn on the table and couch, petals on the bookshelf from a vase of no longer fresh delphiniums, laundry needing to be folded and put away, etc.) was all a preparation, what I was preparing for was not some inspection, the arrival of guests, some point at which I had an appointment, etc., I was preparing instead for preparedness it- self—that being in readiness, which is, in fact, an end in itself, because it provides so much pleasure. My father returned to me in a dream in which he turned to me (I was passing an enormous store, he was standing at the window within, he passed like a ghost through the plate glass, and I introduced him to Larry). There is continuity in incompleteness. I perceive, I interfere—with details repeated and themes dispersed. Wide awake, sipping now and then from a cup of coffee in a saucerless blue and white cup now half gone and half cold beside me, I think that to write is to refigure, though refigura- tion is likewise the work of dreams. The night is never neutral to us. The obvious analogy is with music. We plan an evening out for our evening off and opt to stay in. I feel the same old ambivalence, con- cede as before and as usual hasten home, none of this being new to me. Reality extends into the realm of the apparent and you must consider it. It was eight years ago, in the metaphorical period before the literal Desert Storm that I first heard (from George Lakoff) the term "electronic mail," but it wasn't until five years later, when, thanks to Jalal Toufic I encountered the notion of "the differend" that I could begin to discern the extent of the problem with it. Still, the latitudes don't change their order though spinning the many birds migrating within their solitudes. Philip has remained sardonic but he has become less discontent, Amanda has weathered menopause but has little advice to offer Kate, who remains disdainful, for her part, of Julian's continuing noble hypocrisy, Gil is out of seclusion and playing the violin, Carol has lost weight and Florence has gained it, Dmitri scowls and now speaks seven languages whereas Ralph only speaks local idiolects, and Petra speaks too often and too loudly of her son, but we all lose credibility for awhile now and then. One is not apt to write down trivial anecdotes about merely casual friends. But one can feel the effect of capitalism's increasing control over time, the incremental process of the life being lost. We'd been on side roads for a couple of hours when we pulled into a dirt parking lot outside a small roadside cafe at whose counter a cluster of locals was loudly discussing the blow job. We'd been through sheep fields and confessed, and after we'd dipped our boots in the sink and run knife and fork over their soles, we were shown a confiscated shark penis, a desiccated baboon head, an array of hooves from deer and antelope, and five cans of British beef soup. Sleep says nothing—it has made its break. The dog joined in and tore off the whole of the man's face while the man, his arms clasping it, broke every bone in the dog's body, and there the pair of them lay, near death, each having seized what seemed to be its only chance. Other combinations make sense, too: sentence reasons meaning and meaning sentences reason. "Sentences must stir in a book like leaves in a forest," said Flaubert, "each distinct from each despite their resemblance." Our borders provide us with a theater for exaggeration. Nothing and happily. It is the task of art to preserve disappearance.

*Now long past
beginning, as a
long-term beginner,
I begin*

Again. Afloat, alone, abruptly along. Annoyed. The beginning photographer falls upon objects. She evinces concern for the cognitive state of the poet. It has proved impossible to circumscribe my enthusiasm, I have been curious to learn other people's opinions and I have never been able to remain indifferent to them. Whenever I have an emotion (a sense of affirmation [or, in the broadest sense, love], or fear, frustration, or anger) it means for sure that something is "at stake," there is mattering. Poetry and aboutness and acknowledgement and barbarism and border. Where as a child I used to be afraid of lockjaw with its resemblance to stubbornness, later I feared the madness that filled the gap between what I meant to say and what I did say as it widened. Fins to ears, scales to skin—the harbor bore bees. And now to know the California sisters, painted ladies, monarchs and admirals. One should put one's mind, if to anything, then to one's life (according to Socrates). I attribute to myself what has happened to others, as when, after speculating that it must have been because of a spider bite that my right elbow had become hideously swollen, developing a protuberance the size of a tennis ball, and describing it months later to a friend, suddenly I remembered that it hadn't been my elbow at all that had been affected but L's—and, while I can claim that this propensity is the product of a vivid imagination, it wasn't compassion that had led me to claim that injured elbow for my own but a kind of possessiveness over experience, a greed for experience. We don't begin from a nonchalant blank, beginning is a barrier to that. I'm now armed with a blade but it has to be tempered. I went to see "The Western Mania for Collecting the World," a film. The tenor sang, "In time of war, no one should think of himself," and the soprano threw her spoon down in disgust. Schopenhauer, they say, was a frequent guest because he loved sausage and knowing that he was feared by "the poetical regulars." Pilar?—Johanna?—Dora? My character can proceed without any more name than that of a beginner. Finn. Marka. Window is the name for that which is limited neither to entrance nor exit—and why?—well, because one can smudge it, it is *something*. The sun is in such torrents that I don't go out. It's community, i.e., force of character. There is a future. She'll begin life in the golden house with cobalt trim in Coyoacan whose garden wall cannot keep out the prowling cats kept by the Widow Paz. It is true that life springs only from continuity and equally true that it springs only from discontinuity. My mother said I look at what will follow me and am content. Death, destruction, deduction, Degas, Delacroix, delayed coherence. For one hour each day I will view the world as raw material for my inspiration, my arbitrariness, my needs. Fifteen stamps, not yet designed, will emblemize the decade and bring the century set to its conclusion. The figure I remember will be living a different life from this, not at the beginning and not at the end—those we will share—but now, in the time between. Once each day dysphoria suffuses her, a palm, a sieve, a hollow. Decipher decision. The old writer is neither serene nor exhausted. Those who show disdain for being understood are not the writers of difficult works but the owners of moment. The women sold what they'd sewed and the men in the mines struck. She told me that morale was low, the pace frenzied, there were better jobs she could get, so she had decided to quit her job, but she "couldn't say no," her dismay (fear? guilt?) at "casting negativity into anybody's way" was so extreme that she postponed meeting with her boss week after week, and she works there still. In the gaps between what you want to do, what you think you are doing, and what you do, what exists but you wanted to suppress finds a way in. The water is the spider.   (*139*

And if the full span of the wind-filled sail that we call our attention were allowed to spread, then the shadow it would cast would so darken the currents into which we drive as to render them impenetrable, before and behind as below. Afloat sometimes people hold rocks afloat. The woman who had stumbled at the curb entered the restaurant and once seated she began to cast dice, pitting her left hand against her right. I would rather settle for translations than have all poetry occur in some global poetic language. Behind her the Armenians were playing backgammon. Never use white except for that which the paper provides. There is an as effect. We know people by the things which cause them to change. Through the snow I walked and followed in fading footsteps. I agreed to trade my seat with that of the wife of the man assigned to the seat beside me and moved back two rows to what had been the wife's seat, a middle seat into which I was climbing so as to wedge myself there between a heavy man and a woman with a baby, when I caught the eye of a woman seated across the aisle who smiled and commented, "No good deed goes unpunished." Such displacements alter illusions — which is all to the good. My daughter's two turkeys have been set to rest by her chickens. The hummingbirds in my son's garden are still beset by feral cats that come over the wall from the garden of the poet's widow, but the two eagles that have recently appeared in the highest branches of the cypress tree overlooking the neighborhood appear not to be watching with disinterest. There is a vast field in which to practice for anyone wishing to acquire solid knowledge of what matters. Each film is 10 inches high and 22 inches long and if I could show one it would last 6.6666666 etc. seconds, i.e., forever. The old woman "seeks solitude," her mind "is elsewhere," she "loves to roam in the woods," she "has visions," and she "sings in her sleep." We are not forgetting the patience of the mad, their love
of detail (a cellist in a tree with a microscope and a badger in bed

with a book, etc.) — everyone is out of place in a comedy. One must eliminate fear in order to create a space for living an ethical life. Subjectivity at night must survive hours during which it encounters nothing that is conscious of it and have nothing to judge but itself.

About the Author

Lyn Hejinian is the author of *Happily*, *The Book of a Thousand Eyes*, and *The Language of Inquiry*. She recently received the sixty-sixth Fellowship from The Academy of American Poets for distinguished poetic achievement at mid-career. She lives in Berkeley, California.